CRISIS IN
INDUSTRY

BERTHA DAVIS

CRISIS IN
INDUSTRY

CAN AMERICA
COMPETE?

Franklin Watts
New York / London / Toronto / Sydney
An Impact Book 1989

Photographs courtesy of:
AP/Wide World: pp. 11, 20, 45, 64, 86, 88, 95;
UPI/Bettmann Newsphotos: pp. 39, 67, 99, 102, 125.

Library of Congress Cataloging-in-Publication Data

Davis, Bertha H.
Crisis in industry—can America compete? / Bertha Davis.
p.   cm.—(An impact book)
Bibliography: p.
Includes index.
Summary: Discusses how the United States lost its place as the
dominant economic power of the world due to a host of reasons,
including the entry into the world's markets of highly competitive
foreign products and the poor management of U.S. businesses.
ISBN 0-531-10659-4
1. United States—Economic conditions—1945—Juvenile
literature.   2. United States—Industries—History—20th century—
Juvenile literature.   3. United States—Foreign economic relations—
History—20th century—Juvenile literature.   4. Competition,
International—History—20th century—Juvenile literature.
[1. United States—Economic conditions—1945-   2. United States—
Industries—History—20th century.   3. United States—Foreign
economic relations—History—20th century.   4. Competition,
International—History—20th century.]   I. Title.
HC106.5.D363   1989
338.0973—dc19   88-38584   CIP   AC

CONTENTS

Chapter One
Where We Are
9

Chapter Two
The Trade Deficit:
A Close-up View
15

Chapter Three
The Myth of Deindustrialization
29

Chapter Four
The Global Village
43

Chapter Five
Front-Office Folly
55

Chapter Six
Decline and Turnaround in
the Automobile Industry
61

Chapter Seven
Smokestacks and High Tech
71

Chapter Eight
Trouble in Silicon Valley
83

Chapter Nine
Quality and Other Problems
91

Chapter Ten
How Is Labor Faring?
105

Chapter Eleven
What Role for Government?
115

Glossary
133

Source Notes
137

Index
141

CRISIS IN INDUSTRY

CHAPTER ONE
WHERE
WE ARE

Readers of this book who are under twenty are very likely children of "baby boomers," members of that enormous segment of the nation's population born between 1946 and 1964. Those eighteen years are part of a unique period in American history, a period in which the United States was, without question, the dominant economic power of the world.

The era in which under-twenty readers themselves were born opened in the early 1970s. This, too, is a unique period in American history, but unique in a very different way. In this period in which we live, the United States no longer enjoys the opportunities and discharges the responsibilities associated with economic dominance. Instead, we are a nation grappling with the frustrations and uncertainties associated with loss of dominance.

Does this mean that the United States is no longer the world's largest producer of goods and services? By no means. It still is. Does it no longer buy and sell billions of dollars' worth of goods and services in the world's markets? On the contrary. It is still the world's major trader. Then why the assertion that U.S. dominance has ended?

Because the rest of the world has changed, changed so dramatically that the position of the United States *relative* to the rest of the world is no longer one of dominance. Here's what happened.

When World War II ended in 1945, the United States was the only major industrialized nation whose production facilities had not been damaged. We came out of the war with a larger, stronger industrial base than had existed when we entered the war in 1941. In contrast, much of the productive capacity of Western Europe and Japan had been destroyed.

Concerned by the possibility of communist penetration into countries weakened by the war, the United States adopted as a major foreign policy goal immediately after World War II the rebuilding of Western Europe. To achieve this, vast sums moved abroad under an assistance program called the U.S. Marshall Plan. More dollars went abroad to support military installations maintained by the United States around the world. Still more dollars went abroad as American companies, seeing an unprecedented opportunity to lock in overseas markets, established overseas branches. Thus, the dollar became an international currency—wanted everywhere, accepted everywhere.

Those American dollars were largely used to buy products made by American producers. After all, who was there, in the early postwar years, to compete with them? That uncontested competitive position was an enormous stimulus to the American economy; those were golden years of prosperity for American business.

By the late 1950s, Western European companies, their new or reconstructed factories equipped with the most technologically advanced machines and equipment and operated with the most sophisticated American know-how—for American technology as well as American dollars went abroad—were reentering the world's markets. The reconstruction of Japan, sponsored under American occupation and spurred by Japan's role as a

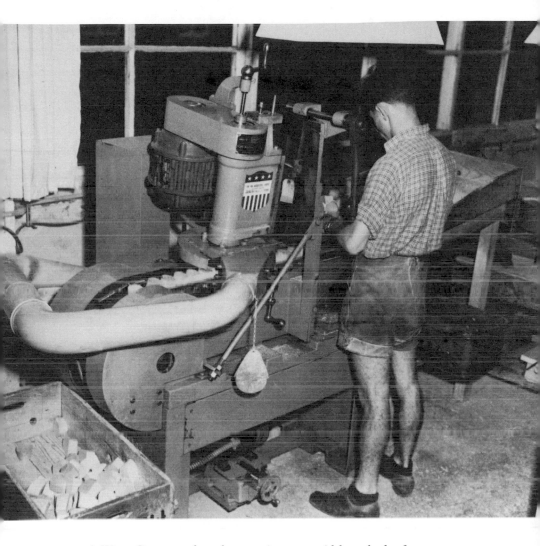

A West German shoe factory in 1952. Although the factory was about 30 percent destroyed in World War II, by 1952 production was slightly higher than its prewar output, in part due to American machine tools brought into the country under the Marshall Plan. The heel-making machine seen here still bears the Marshall Plan label.

supply base during the Korean and Vietnam wars, very soon created competitors there.

At first, the position of the United States vis-à-vis foreign challengers seemed impregnable. The ability of U.S. producers to compete in world markets was taken for granted. They were supplying more than one-fourth of all the exports of manufactured goods that entered world trade, and they seemed to have the home market virtually locked up. Ninety-eight percent of the U.S. market for manufactured goods was supplied, in 1960, by American producers.

There were some, however, who saw the handwriting on the wall. Concern that the U.S. position in world markets was likely to change was voiced as far back as the Kennedy administration. In the Nixon administration, a study of the nation's competitive position in the world indicated that such a change was already under way.[1] The study showed that between 1960 and 1970, U.S. share of total world exports fell from 18.2 percent to 15.4 percent; its share of world manufactured exports fell from 22.8 percent to 18.4 percent. That was just the beginning.

During the years of U.S. economic dominance, over half of all the goods and services produced in the entire world was produced in the United States; 22 percent of all the world's trade was carried on by the United States. Of the ten biggest banks in the world, seven were U.S. banks. By 1982, the number of U.S. banks in the top ten was two; U.S. share of world production was barely 25 percent; its share of the world's trade was down to 9½ percent. The home market was under seige. When foreign competitors first entered the U.S. postwar domestic market, only a small number of U.S.-made products were threatened. By 1986, foreign products were competing with 78 percent of American-made goods. Inroads of imports became so great that year after year in this decade the amount that "we owe them'' has exceeded by billions the amount that ''they owe us.'' The trade deficit has been headline news.

Competition from Western Europe and Japan plus new competition from the so-called tigers of southeastern Asia—South Korea, Taiwan, Singapore, and Hong Kong—not to mention Mexico and Brazil, have unquestionably changed the position of the United States in relation to the rest of the world, and the trade deficit signals that change dramatically. The results of burgeoning imports and far from burgeoning exports, results in terms of weakened industries and pockets of unemployment, were so disturbing in the 1980s that ''how to restore American competitiveness'' became a major political issue. In one year some five thousand bills on the subject were introduced in Congress. So politically essential did it become to be involved in the big ''C'' issue that one Washington insider, asked what Congress was doing about American competitiveness, made the somewhat cynical observation that ''Washington is doing what it does to all hot new ideas. It's hugging it to death.''

Tackling the issue of American competitiveness that is signaled by the trade deficit is no easy task, for the deficit is a *symptom*, not itself a disease. Behind the symptom, causing the symptom, is a tangle of troublesome problems. But to explore the question raised in this book—Can America compete in the world market?—the symptom must be the starting point.

CHAPTER TWO
THE TRADE DEFICIT: A CLOSE-UP VIEW

When Americans sell more to foreigners than they buy from foreigners, exports exceed imports; there is a trade surplus. When Americans buy more from foreigners than they sell to foreigners, imports exceed exports; there is a trade deficit.

Many kinds of transactions other than the purchase and sale of goods enter into the international account books. Banks, insurance companies, communication and transportation companies provide services; individuals, businesses, and governments invest in property and securities; tourists travel. In these transactions, if "we pay them," the transaction is, in effect, an import. If "they pay us," the transaction is, in effect, an export. The amounts involved in these so-called invisible exports and invisible imports are substantial, and they have an important place in the *Current Account*, the international transactions balance sheet, of the United States. Since so much attention is given to U.S. *trade* with Japan, it is interesting to note that the balance of *invisible* imports versus *invisible* exports is substantially in our nation's favor because Japanese companies pay large royalties to U.S. companies for use of American technology and sales to Japanese by U.S. companies based in Japan substantially exceed sales of Japanese businesses based in the United States to Americans.

Far more significant in the Current Account are the amounts involved in the export and import of *goods*. Those amounts are the figures that produce the *trade balance*. This was the trade balance in 1987:

Merchandise imports (billions)		Merchandise exports (billions)		Trade deficit (billions)
411.3	−	257.6	=	153.7

WHY THE TRADE DEFICIT MATTERS— THE BIG PICTURE

Knowledgeable people look at the trade deficit as part of a bigger picture. They understand that the deficit sends this message: Except for the exports bought by foreigners, American consumers, American producers, and American governments (federal, state, local) are using up *all* the goods and services the United States produces. Repeat—all of it. In addition, they are using up the billions of dollars' worth of imports represented by the trade deficit. In a nutshell: The United States is consuming more than it is producing. To reduce the trade deficit, therefore, the nation must produce more or consume less. Most people agree that the first option is the more desirable one. Producing more means more jobs, a rising standard of living. Nobody likes the second option. It means a falling standard of living.

Most people have not yet faced up to these alternatives. They haven't had to. It is possible, for a while, to take care of the difference between what "we owe them" for imports and what "they owe us" for exports by going deeper and deeper into debt. That is the option the United States has chosen, thus resulting in the nation's status as the world's largest debtor.

UPS AND DOWNS OF
THE TRADE BALANCE

The graph on page 18 shows that the U.S. trade balance has gone through three stages in the post–World War II years. In the first stage, from 1950 to 1976, the range of fluctuations in the trade balance was narrow; most years showed modest surpluses; the deficits of 1971, 1972, and 1974 were exceptions. In the second stage, from 1977 to 1981, trade deficits were persistent but not enormous. Although imports exceeded exports each year, both were growing at about the same rate.

The steadily climbing imports of the 1970s are clear evidence of unprecedented competition from foreign producers in the American domestic market, a market that not too long before had been absolutely dominated by American producers. The textile, shoe, and automobile industries were particularly hard hit by that competition. The steadily climbing exports of the 1970s, on the other hand, conceal the fact that there was trouble there, too. In some industries that depend heavily on exports to keep them profitable, foreign competitors made serious inroads into the overseas market shares of American exporters. Exports of power-generating and agricultural machinery, for example, dropped substantially.

Plant closings and displacement of workers in industries hurt by imports or loss of overseas markets received more and more media coverage. As those stories began to capture public attention, the ability of American producers to compete in the world market began to be questioned. As observers of the business scene watched for foreign orders that did not come in and saw the foreign cars that did come in, in steadily increasing num-

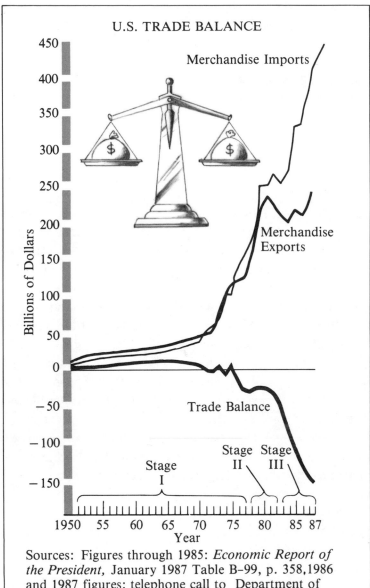

U.S. TRADE BALANCE

Billions of Dollars

450
400
350
300
250
200
150
100
50
0
−50
−100
−150

Merchandise Imports

Merchandise Exports

Trade Balance

Stage I

Stage II

Stage III

1950 55 60 65 70 75 80 85 87

Year

Sources: Figures through 1985: *Economic Report of the President,* January 1987 Table B–99, p. 358, 1986 and 1987 figures: telephone call to Department of Commerce, Bureau of Economic Analysis, June 7, 1988.

bers, books and magazine articles began to prophesy the "deindustrialization of America."

In the third stage of the trade-balance story, from 1982 to 1986, the situation worsened seriously. Exports actually declined in 1982 and 1983 and did not get back to 1981 levels until 1987. Imports dipped only once, in 1982, and after rebounding in 1983, kept climbing. The trade deficit mounted to unprecedented heights.

The stage we are now in opened in 1987 with a deficit of $153.7 billion. Higher than the 1986 deficit, it concealed the turnaround in trade that actually began in 1987. More about that later.

THE NUTS AND BOLTS
OF FOREIGN TRADE

Anyone who has visited a foreign country knows that an American must buy *pounds* to travel in Great Britain and *pesetas* to travel in Spain. The same principle applies when Americans buy goods from other countries. Each article bought from abroad (imported) must be paid for in the currency of the country in which it was purchased. To get the pounds, pesetas, yen, or francs needed to pay for their travels or purchases, Americans must buy them with dollars.

The reverse, of course, is also true. Foreigners who travel in the United States or buy goods from the United States must supply themselves with dollars. They must buy dollars with their pounds, pesetas, yen, or francs.

Exchange rates for the dollar reflect the value of the dollar in relation to the currencies of other countries. For example: Suppose on February 1 an American who needs yen can buy 140 yen with one dollar; a Japanese who needs dollars can buy one dollar with 140 yen. Suppose on February 28 an American

An American visitor to Tokyo converts dollars to yen. The exchange rate on this particular day, April 19, 1986, was 171.15 yen for a dollar.

who needs yen can buy only 120 yen with one dollar; a Japanese who needs dollars can buy one dollar with only 120 yen. The value of the dollar went down during February; the value of the yen went up.

The number of yen one can buy with a dollar or the number of francs it takes to buy a dollar—the dollar/yen exchange rate, the franc/dollar exchange rate—changes over time. Some exchange rates are extremely volatile, some much less so. Volatility is increased by the trading that goes on in the $200 billion per day currency market. Foreign-exchange traders buy and sell dollars, pounds, yen, whatever, not to pay for purchases of goods or services but simply to make profits on small rate differences from place to place. Only one-twentieth, $4 trillion, of the $80 trillion currency exchange transactions in a year are related to trade in goods and services.

THE DOLLAR AND
THE TRADE DEFICIT

It is important for the U.S. government, the business community, and many individuals to track the overall value of the dollar from day to day, year to year. To make such tracking possible, the Federal Reserve Board, which supervises the U.S. banking system, publishes a *trade-weighted value of the dollar index number* based on exchange rates for the ten countries that are the nation's most important trading partners. The words "trade-weighted" mean that the exchange rates for our most important trading partners count more heavily in the average than the rates of the less important.

The board uses the year 1973 as the year to which other years are compared. The weighted average of the exchange rates of that year is called *100*. When the exchange rates for other years are fed into the computer, it produces index numbers, higher or lower than 100, that show how much the overall value of the dollar rose or fell against the ten tracked currencies. An average index number for any given month or year can readily be computed from the daily figures.

Here's what happened to the value of the dollar during the years when the merchandise trade deficit began to grow to problem proportions: 1974—101.4; 1975—98.5; 1976—105.6; 1977—103.3; 1978—92.4; 1979—88.1; 1980—87.4. Nothing startling in those fluctuations, but look at these dollar values: 1981—102.9; 1982—116.6; 1983—125.3; 1984—138.3; 1985—143.2.[2]

A dramatic surge in a currency's value like that shown above inevitably raises the issue of why it happened. The most generally accepted explanation for the dollar's rise in the 1980s is the U.S. budget deficits of those years. The deficits made it necessary for the United States to borrow heavily by selling treasury bills and bonds. These securities were very attractive to foreigners in the 1980s. They were absolutely safe, and they paid higher rates of interest than comparable investments available to many foreign investors in their own countries. To buy treasury issues, or any other attractive high-interest-paying American securities, foreigners had to buy dollars. Heavy demand for dollars pushed up the prices for dollars—exchange rates. The rising dollar index numbers reflect those rising rates.

When trade-deficit figures for the 1980s are placed next to dollar-value figures for the same years, it seems reasonable to conclude that there is some connection between them:

	Value of the Dollar 1973 = 100	Trade Deficit ($ billions)
1983	125.3	67.1
1984	138.3	112.5
1985	143.2	124.4

And there is a connection.

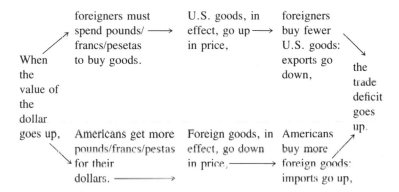

This is not just theory. There is general agreement among government, business, and academic experts that the rise in the value of the dollar in the 1980s was a major cause of the burgeoning trade deficit.

PRESSURE TO DO SOMETHING

As might be expected, the trade deficit, plant closings, displaced workers, and the challenge to American competitiveness became political issues in the 1980s. Activists aware of the big picture urged long-range policies to promote growth. Many personally involved in hard-hit industries favored a more direct approach, urging the appealing—because readily understandable—remedy that the United States "do something about imports." This in turn aroused fears that some kind of protectionist legislation would be pushed through Congress. Such legislation is repeatedly urged by industries hurt by imports, but it is universally opposed by those who understand that the evils that flow from protectionist legislation—retaliation by other nations, for example—far outweigh the distress that spawns its passage.

So, partly to avert pressure for protection, the government began efforts to bring the value of the dollar down. Actually the dollar did fall slightly in February 1985, but the index continued to hover in the 140 range. So representatives of the United States met in September 1985 with representatives of four other major trading nations: West Germany, Japan, Britain, and France. Out of that meeting came an agreement that they would work together to bring the dollar down to a point where U.S. goods would be more competitive in foreign markets and foreign goods less competitive here. Similar meetings with these and other countries were held in subsequent years to ward off the possibility that the dollar's fall would involve a crash landing.

DECLINE AND
DISAPPOINTMENT

The dollar's value did drop from 1985 on, and the Federal Reserve index was fluctuating just over 100 in early 1987. The index, because it is an average, did not reveal variations in the degree of change among the ten index countries. As the graph on page 25 shows, the fall in value of the dollar against the Japanese yen and the West German mark was spectacular, whereas there was no dramatic change in the exchange rate for some other important U.S. trading partners: Canada, notably, as well as Mexico, Brazil, Taiwan, South Korea, Singapore, and Hong Kong.

Bringing down the value of the dollar is intended to affect the trade balance by making U.S. goods cheaper for foreigners, and foreign goods more expensive for Americans. The decline

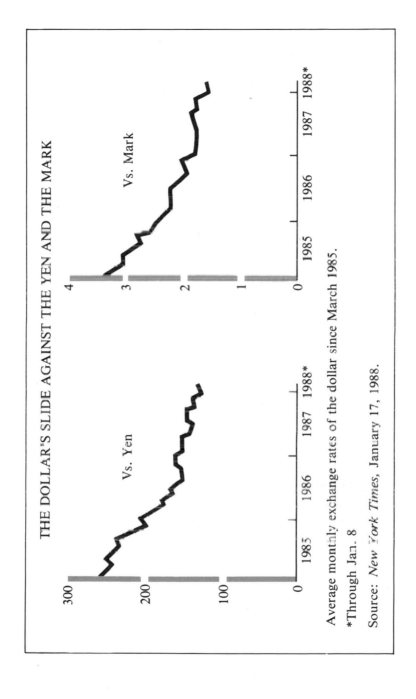

THE DOLLAR'S SLIDE AGAINST THE YEN AND THE MARK

Vs. Yen

Vs. Mark

Average monthly exchange rates of the dollar since March 1985.

*Through Jan. 8

Source: *New York Times*, January 17, 1988.

of the dollar that began in February 1985 produced some of the anticipated results. With lower dollar prices as bait, American producers stepped up their efforts to sell overseas; exports did rise. Prices of many imports did rise; imports flattened out. Since Japan accounts for almost one-third of the trade deficit, it was good news when the price of Japanese cars went up about $2,000 and sales did drop. While Japan's purchases of U.S. goods did not surge, the high-valued yen gave cash-rich Japanese such an advantage in U.S. real estate markets that one observer likened their huge purchases of U.S. property to buying with "play money."

But all was not well. On the basis of past experience, prices should have reflected 100 percent of the exchange-rate changes within two years. They did not. Between March 1985 and September 1987 the value of the dollar went down 28.8 percent; import prices (not including oil) went up only 18.8 percent.[3] Clearly there had been no 100 percent pass-through. When the trade-deficit figures for the second quarter (April–June) of 1987 came in at $41 billion, followed by a record-breaking monthly deficit of $16.5 billion in July, the numbers were viewed with great alarm. Headlines proclaimed that the declining dollar was not correcting the trade deficit.

REAL VERSUS NOMINAL
TRADE BALANCES

Actually the declining dollar was doing a better job than the numbers suggested. Dollar trade balances, in the early stages of a turnaround, often conceal what is really happening. Consider this situation:

Month 1   Ten units of exports are sold at $100 per unit for a total of $1,000.

Month 2   Value of dollar goes down and export
           prices fall.

Month 3   Twelve units of exports are sold at $80
           per unit for a total of $960.

If one looks only at the *nominal* (dollar-value) figure for exports—and that is the figure reported in the newspapers—one would conclude that exports went down in Month 3. Bad news. *Real* exports (in terms of volume—units sent out of the country) went up in Month 3. Good news, but not publicized.

Import figures usually yield the same kind of distorted picture in an early turnaround stage:

Month 1   Fifteen units of imports are bought at $100
           per unit for a total of $1,500.

Month 2   Value of dollar goes down, and import
           prices rise.

Month 3   Nine units of imports are bought at $120
           per unit for a total of $1,560.

Nominal imports continued to rise (bad news), although real imports had started going down (unpublicized good news).

In other words, it takes a while for an increased volume of exports at lower prices to work its way through to increased nominal exports and for a decreased volume of imports at higher prices to work its way through to decreased nominal imports. Volume—real—figures are important because it's the volume of exports, the number or amount of items that must be made to fill foreign orders, that affects employment in U.S. factories. But the dollar trade balance is just as important because it shows whether the United States is going further into debt, reducing its debt, breaking even, or beginning to build a trade-balance surplus.

A CONTINUING STORY

While the total trade deficit for 1987 was higher than that for 1986, the figures for the later months of the year showed clearly that an upturn in exports was under way. The first quarter of 1988 maintained the upward trend of exports and suggested some moderating of the rise of imports. The figures for the first quarter were:

Merchandise exports $75.7 billion[4]
Merchandise imports   109.9 billion

On the basis of those first quarter figures, the Department of Commerce projected these totals for 1988: merchandise exports of $302.9 billion, which would signal an impressive rise in exports; merchandise imports of $439.7 billion, which would signal persisting interest in foreign products. The resulting projected trade deficit of $136.8 billion, if it materializes, will be an encouraging improvement over 1987. But it would still be far too high to warrant complacency.

The trade deficit is a controversial issue, but some degree of consensus seems to prevail on these points:

- The trade deficit will not disappear in the near future.

- Manipulating the value of the dollar should not be relied upon as the major strategy for achieving improvement in the trade balance.

- A gradual, steady decline is acceptable.

- Substantially increased exports of manufactured goods will and should play an important part in reducing the deficit. The deindustrialization of the U.S. economy, in other words, is being recognized as a myth.

CHAPTER THREE

THE MYTH OF DEINDUSTRIALIZATION

About 110 million people in the United States are employed. Their jobs are so varied that there are over thirty-five thousand entries—from Abalone Diver to Zyler Mounter—in the *Dictionary of Occupational Titles*. Varied as individual jobs are, the businesses in which they are performed can be grouped to yield a meaningful overall picture of the American economy. The classification system shown on page 30 is the one used by the Census Bureau; there are many others.

The bureau's classification assigns jobs to three major sectors: the agriculture sector, the goods-producing sector, and the service (non-goods-producing) sector. The agriculture sector includes, in addition to farm workers, those employed in forestry and fisheries; the goods-producing sector includes workers engaged in mining, construction, and manufacturing; the service sector, as the chart shows, includes a wide variety of activities.

ANNOUNCEMENT
OF A TURNING POINT

Employment in manufacturing dropped significantly between 1973 and 1980, particularly in the automobile industry. This devel-

INDUSTRY CLASSIFICATION

Agriculture Sector

Goods–Producing Sector

Mining

Construction

Manufacturing

Service–Producing Sector

Transportation, communication, and public utilities

Trade

Wholesale
Retail

Finance, insurance, and real estate

Services

Business services

Advertising
Consumer credit reporting and collection
Mailing, reproduction, and stenographic services
Services to buildings: cleaning, maintenance
Personnel supply
Computer and data processing
Miscellaneous: R&D, management and consulting, protection

Personal services
Entertainment and recreation
Professional services

Health
Education
Legal
Welfare and religious

Public administration

Postal
Other federal
State
Local

Source: Michael Urquhart, ''The employment shift to services: where did it come from?'' *Monthly Labor Review,* April 1984, pp.15-22.

opment, plus the obvious upheaval going on in other industries of the Midwest, led a number of industry analysts to conclude that a fundamental change was taking place in the American economy, a change as significant as that revealed by the census of 1910.[5] That census produced the startling finding that there were more blue-collar—manual, industrial—workers in the labor force than farm workers. In every previous census agricultural workers had been the largest occupational group in the United States.

Analysts of the 1970s argued that a similar structural change was taking place: that the United States was shifting from an industrial to a service economy; that the deindustrialization of America was under way. Along with this conclusion came, from many quarters, the recommendation that the United States accept the inevitability of this change, let its smokestack industries die, and concentrate on strengthening high-tech manufacturing and service industries.

DEINDUSTRIALIZATION
REFUTED

This line of thinking gained fairly wide acceptance for a while. President Reagan, for example, expressed the opinion of many when he said that "the progression of an economy such as America's from agriculture to manufacturing to services is a natural change." Today it is generally accepted that manufacturing is alive and determined to stay alive. Even once-devoted advocates of structural change now agree that the challenge facing the United States is not to make a rapid transition from smokestack industry to high-tech industry and services. They recognize that the real challenge lies in the answer to this question: How quickly can we bring high technology to smokestack industries?

31

There are several reasons for the shift in thinking. In the first place, developments in the early 1980s proved that expanding high-tech industries could not replace ailing smokestack industries. Disastrous inroads of foreign competition—notably in the computer-chip industry—raised the specter that Silicon Valley, California's symbol of high tech, might become a Rust Bowl.

Second, the notion that a service sector could flourish without a robust manufacturing sector was soon recognized as a fallacy. The volume of activity in transportation, wholesale and retail trade, financial and business services, insurance, all part of the service sector, is clearly linked to the volume of manufacturing activity.

Third, the so-called defense argument remains impressive. The national security interests of the United States would be ill served if the decline of manufacturing were to make the nation dependent on outside sources for such basic products as steel and machine tools.

Finally, the manufacturing sector has traditionally included more high-wage jobs than the service sector. While there are many very high wage jobs in services, there are very many more low-wage jobs. It is generally agreed that a broad shift of jobs into the service sector would mean, overall, a lowering of workers' income.

The theoretical case in support of deindustrialization has just about collapsed; production statistics make clear that it is not happening. As the figures on page 33 show, the *number of workers* employed in manufacturing has declined; so has the *percentage* of manufacturing workers in the total nonagricultural labor force. But the contribution of manufacturing to the gross national product has remained with remarkable consistency between 20 and 22 percent. How could fewer manufacturing workers do this? Their *productivity* increased.

EMPLOYMENT IN MANUFACTURING

	Number of Workers (thousands)	Percentage of Total Non–Agricultural Employment
1959	16,675	31.3
1969	20,167	28.7
1979	21,040	23.4
1980	20,285	22.4
1981	20,170	22.1
1982	19,878	22.3
1983	18,434	20.4
1984	19,378	20.5
1985	19,260	19.7
1986	18,965	19.1
1987	19,065	18.6

Sources: Ronald E. Kutscher and Valerie A. Personick, "Deindustrialization and the Shift to Services," *Monthly Labor Review,* June 1986, pp. 3–13; Telephone call to Department of Labor, Bureau of Labor Statistics, June 10, 1988.

PRODUCTIVITY—KEY
TO COMPETITIVENESS

America's ability to compete hinges on America's productivity. What productivity is, how it can be increased, how U.S. productivity compares with that of other nations—these matters must be explored.

Productivity means output per work hour. Rising productivity means an increase in output per work hour; a decline in productivity means a decrease in output per work hour. The *rate* of productivity growth or decline is a percentage that shows how rapidly or slowly output per work hour is changing. Here is an example.

Assume that in Year 1 the ABC Company's ten workers work five seven-hour days, a total of 350 work hours. Assume that in those 350 work hours they produce 700 widgets. They work at this rate throughout the year. Assume that in Year 2 the same ten workers, using the same equipment, produce 770 widgets in 350 work hours. Widget production increased by 70; output rose to 2.2 widgets per work hour, a 10 percent increase over Year 1. Productivity of the ABC Company, in other words, rose at the rate of 10 percent.

Since the workers in Year 2 were using the same equipment as in Year 1, something related to the workers themselves must have changed. Perhaps they were more efficiently organized; perhaps they received some additional training; perhaps their morale and motivation improved because of the introduction of a bonus or profit-sharing plan.

Consider another situation. Assume that in Year 1 the XYZ Company's 100 workers, on a 35-hour work week (3,500 work hours) produce 35,000 gadgets, an output of 10 gadgets per work hour. In Year 2 the number of workers has been reduced to 50, and new machines have been installed. Working with the new machines, 50 workers produced, in their 1,750 work hours, the same number of gadgets as 100 workers produced in Year 1. In other words, output rose to 20 gadgets per work hour; productivity increased at the rate of 100 percent.

From these two examples it appears that manufacturers can increase productivity by raising the efficiency of their workers; they can increase productivity by installing new, technologically more advanced machinery (add to their capital investment). Productivity can be increased by workers who work smarter, by machines that work smarter, or by a combination of smarter workers using smarter machines.

The link between productivity and ability to compete is clear. Going back to widgets, assume that in Year 1 it cost the ABC Company $7,000 per week to turn out 700 widgets. Cost of production per widget was $10. When productivity increased in Year 2 and output per week rose to 770 widgets, cost of production per widget fell to about $9.09. This drop in cost per unit enabled the ABC Company to compete with an imported widget, priced at $9.50, that had been taking over the widget market.

WHERE THE
UNITED STATES STANDS

Productivity can be measured and expressed in many ways. For a specific industry, it can be measured in terms of the work hours that go into a unit of product. For example, in the most efficient steel plants, production of a ton of steel requires four work hours; in the least efficient, the formula is nine work hours per ton. The direction in which a nation's productivity is moving and the rate at which change is taking place is expressed in plus or minus percentages. Thus, one country's rate of productivity change can be compared to the rates of other countries; one country's rate of productivity change can be tracked over a period of years. There is another way to make comparisons. It involves dividing a nation's GNP, which is a dollar figure—or a yen, pound, mark, or franc figure translated into dollars—by the total number of hours worked in that nation. This yields a dollar figure for output per work hour.

The graph below and on the facing page show how the United States fares in both types of comparisons, rate of productivity change and output per work hour. The contrast is startling. The United States is the most productive nation in the world. But productivity is *growing faster* in other industrial or industrializing nations. One U.S. productivity expert predicts that Canada, France, Norway, West Germany, Belgium, and Japan will eventually move ahead of the United States.[6]

It is reasonable, of course, for the United States to have had a lower *rate* of productivity growth in the 1970s and 1980s

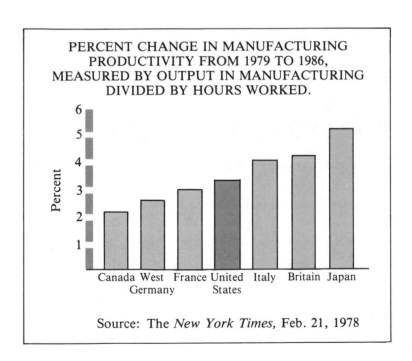

PERCENT CHANGE IN MANUFACTURING PRODUCTIVITY FROM 1979 TO 1986, MEASURED BY OUTPUT IN MANUFACTURING DIVIDED BY HOURS WORKED.

Source: The *New York Times,* Feb. 21, 1978

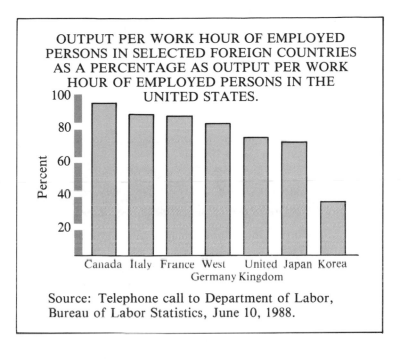

OUTPUT PER WORK HOUR OF EMPLOYED
PERSONS IN SELECTED FOREIGN COUNTRIES
AS A PERCENTAGE AS OUTPUT PER WORK
HOUR OF EMPLOYED PERSONS IN THE
UNITED STATES.

Canada Italy France West United Japan Korea
Germany Kingdom

Source: Telephone call to Department of Labor,
Bureau of Labor Statistics, June 10, 1988.

than countries that are newly emerging on the industrial scene.
If a country starts from an extremely low output-per-work-hour
figure, increases in that figure translate into impressive productivity growth rates.

While it is useful to look at U.S. productivity figures from
that perspective, nonetheless two disquieting facts must be faced:
the rate at which U.S. productivity is now growing is lower
than it has been in the past; the rate at which U.S. productivity
is growing is lower than that of its industrial rivals.

One further point must be made concerning U.S. productivity. Gains in productivity have varied enormously among the
three major sectors of the economy. The growth of productivity
in agriculture has been phenomenal. The service sector presents
a distressing contrast. The non-goods-producing industries have
poured billions of dollars of capital investment into their banks,

transportation lines, and offices to provide them with the most modern high-tech equipment available. Despite this, productivity growth in the service sector has averaged less than half a percentage point per year since 1979.

Productivity growth in manufacturing slowed down seriously in the 1970s. That fact, which signaled serious weaknesses in American manufacturing, plus the rising strength of foreign manufacturers, plus the rise in the value of the dollar produced the decline in American competitiveness that helped to build the trade deficit to alarming proportions.

THE TASK AHEAD

Knowledgeable people agree on these points:

- Decline in the value of the dollar will increase exports and decrease imports. It has already done so to a degree, as we have seen. But the dollar cannot do the whole job of restoring American competitiveness.

- In the years ahead, the pressure from foreign manufacturers will increase, not decrease.

- Therefore, if American manufacturers are to sell more abroad and win back domestic customers from foreign

In an effort to stem the tide of foreign imports, American manufacturers urged shoppers to "buy American." Here tags bearing MADE IN U.S.A. are being inspected for flaws.

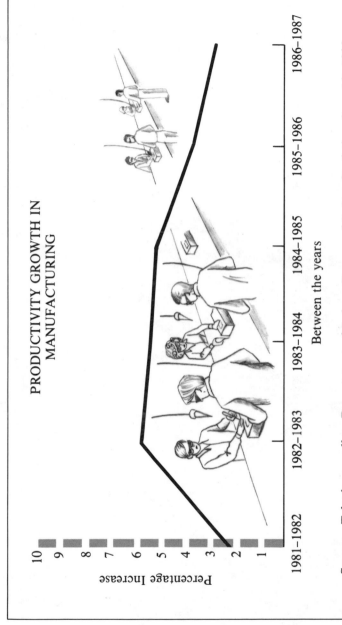

PRODUCTIVITY GROWTH IN MANUFACTURING

Percentage Increase

10
9
8
7
6
5
4
3
2
1

1981–1982 1982–1983 1983–1984 1984–1985 1985–1986 1986–1987

Between the years

Source: Telephone call to Department of Labor, Bureau of Labor Statistics, June 10, 1988.

competitors, they must improve their performance. Manufacturing productivity figures for the eighties, as shown on page 40, suggest that they are on the way, but they have a long way to go.

Analysis of what went wrong in American manufacturing and what's starting to go right must begin with a look at the new global village in which all this is happening.

CHAPTER FOUR
THE GLOBAL VILLAGE

Natural gas owned by Indonesia's oil agency, Pertamina, flows out of a well discovered by Royal Dutch Shell into a liquification plant designed by French engineers and built by a Korean construction company. The liquified gas is loaded onto U.S.-flag tankers, built in U.S. yards after a Norwegian design. The ships shuttle to Japan and deliver the liquid gas to a Japanese public utility, which uses it to produce electricity that powers an electronic factory making television sets that are shipped aboard a Hong Kong-owned container ship to California for sale to American farmers in Louisiana who grow rice that is sold to Indonesia and shipped there aboard Greek-flag bulk carriers.

All of the various facilities, ships, products, and services involved in the complex series of events are financed by U.S., European, and Japanese commercial banks, working in some cases with international and local governmental agencies. These facilities, ships, products, and services are insured and reinsured by U.S., European, and Japanese insurance companies. Investors in these facilities, ships, products, and services are

located throughout the world. This illustration is not only fac-
tual, it is typical of transactions that take place over and over
again daily throughout the globe.[7]

Politically, of course, the world is divided, obviously and dan-
gerously so. But the economic world—the world of producing
goods and services, buying and selling them, using them to
satisfy wants or produce other goods—that world is a very different matter. In that economic world, one business executive
asserts, "the boundaries that separate one nation from another
are no more real than the equator." Exaggeration to make a
point, of course, for boundaries are often barriers in the economic world. But the global perspective implied in the observation is real in modern business.

THE MULTINATIONALS

A fourteen-year-old who assembles transistor radios in a Hong
Kong factory, a waitress in a German hotel, a teacher of typing
in Mexico, and an accountant in New York City all work for
the same company. How can that be possible? Easily. The company is a multinational conglomerate, one of the giant corporations that dominate today's business world. The "conglomerate" part of the label means that the corporation is involved
with producing and selling a variety of goods and services. The
"multinational" part of the label means that while the corporation is organized under the laws of one nation, it does business
in many nations.

Business firms buying and selling in distant lands is nothing
new. The history of trade is almost as long as the history of
humankind. Overseas factories to serve overseas markets, while
a recent development by comparison, go back well over a hundred
years.

The day shift at Kyocera International's San Diego plant begins with calisthenics and inspirational speeches. The plant turns out 70 percent of ceramic semiconductor packaging made in the United States. Its parent company is Kyoto Ceramic of Japan.

But today's global corporations are different from the world-ranging producers and traders of earlier years. Yesterday's operators on the world scene viewed their overseas activities as adjuncts or extensions of their home-based activities. Today, global corporate executives view the world as the basic corporate arena; they think and act in terms of a global source for what they wish to buy, a global factory, a global market—a global village.

Without communications technology to support it, such a world view could not be implemented, but the technology exists. Texas Instruments, Inc., for example, an American multinational, links, via space satellite, its thirty or so thousand computer terminals in forty different countries. Modern banking facilities make possible the transfer, in seconds, of billions of dollars or other currencies among the units of a multinational empire.

A list of the world's giant multinationals would include about 450 corporations. Most are American, but Great Britain, the Netherlands, West Germany, France, Switzerland, Italy, Canada, Sweden, and Japan have also spawned giants. In 1986, the 50 biggest multinationals had sales of $1.3 trillion; they employed 8.7 million people. U.S. multinationals account for two-thirds or more of U.S. industrial output.

WHY TRADE HAPPENS

In an earlier day, trade happened because nations wanted things that could not be grown, mined, or manufactured within their borders. In other words, trade resulted from natural or technological advantages that some nations enjoyed over others. Differences among nations based on unique control of natural resources continue to give rise to much of the world's trade. But differences in technological progress are blurring. The developed nations of the world are becoming more and more alike in technology and production processes; the newly industrializing countries are moving rapidly toward the same level. As one analyst puts it, a "globalization of technology" has taken place. Increasingly today it is the decisions of global corporations rather than comparative advantage that determine what will be produced where and thus how trade will flow.

A HYPOTHETICAL CASE

Consider the Giant Computer Corporation (GCC), a hypothetical multinational based in the United States. GCC decides to enter the market for personal computers in Newlandia. As vigorous sales efforts produce increasing orders, GCC management considers these options:

- It can continue to fill orders from Newlandia from its factories in the United States, expanding them if necessary. Or,

- It can enter into an arrangement with Newtex, a Newlandia corporation, under which Newtex will be licensed to use GCC technology to produce and sell GCC personal computers in Newlandia. Royalty and profit-sharing clauses in the contract will assure GCC's return on Newlandia business. Or,

- GCC can build a plant in Newlandia, import personal computer components from the United States, assemble them, and sell them to customers in Newlandia. Or,

- GCC can have the Newlandia plant produce personal computer components as well as assemble them. Or,

- GCC can have components for the Newlandia plant produced in Pacifica, a country nearer to Newlandia than the United States. Or,

- GCC can use its Newlandia plant not only to fill orders from that country but also orders from other countries, including orders from U.S. customers.

Choices among these options are governed by one simple criterion: What course of action will produce the maximum profit from the corporation's worldwide operations. As one U.S. auto executive explained his choice between an American and a Japanese supplier: "Quality, cost and delivery speed [factors which affect company profits] are the real issues, not nationality."[8]

A REAL CASE—THE AUTOMOBILE INDUSTRY

GCC is a hypothetical corporation, but it is an accurate model. Consider who makes what where in the automobile industry. One GM car is made from end to end in Japan and imported by Chevrolet for sale in the U.S. market. Another "American" car is assembled in California by American union workers in a factory that is jointly owned by Toyota and GM and managed by Toyota executives. Some Ford cars have engines made in Japan; one GM model is powered by an engine from Brazil; Mitsubishi motors are in a wide range of Chrysler models; a high-priced Chrysler or Cadillac sports car may start life in the United States, go to Italy to have the body added, then return to the United States for final assembly.

The first foreign cars that entered the United States were made abroad and imported. That pattern now accounts for about one-quarter of U.S. car sales. But in addition, many foreign cars are now assembled in the United States: Hondas in Ohio and California, Mazdas in Michigan, Toyotas in Kentucky.

When Japanese automobile companies began assembling cars intended for the U.S. market in the United States, the engines, transmissions, and other major parts were imported from Japan. Then Japanese parts plants in the United States began producing those components. Then those U.S.-based Japanese producers of components began negotiating with U.S. automobile companies to supply components for American cars: air conditioners are available from a Japanese plant in Battle Creek, Michigan; motor mounts from another Japanese plant in Livonia, Michigan; steering wheels from still another Japanese supplier based in Eaton, Ohio; tires from a Japanese supplier in Tennessee.

In 1987 there were fewer than 30 Japanese parts makers operating in the United States. Estimates of a rise to 300 such plants by 1990 come from both American and Japanese industry analysts.[9] Plans for additional Japanese assembly plants in the United States are also well under way. Clearly the multinational automobile companies of the world take the global view as they decide where to buy what is needed to make their cars and where their cars should be assembled.

OTHER INDUSTRIES

Manufacture of television sets was solely an enterprise of pioneer American producers as late as 1948. By the mid-1950s, with the market for TV sets vastly expanded, a second group of American producers had entered the industry. The original producers, pushed by this new competition, built plants abroad, first to serve local overseas markets, then to export to other countries. After Japan gained a dominant position in the industry, largely with technology leased from U.S. firms, no TV sets were produced by American manufacturers in the United States.

49

As wages began to rise in Japan, some TV production was moved to South Korea. Westinghouse TVs are made in Canada and Japan, Emerson radios in Taiwan, General Instruments' TV tuners come from Portugal and Taiwan. Japanese produce TV sets in California and Arkansas. To round out the circle, one American multinational recently transferred some TV production from South Korea back to a plant in Indiana. GE cassette recorders, microwave ovens, and room air conditioners are made in Asia; Kodak's 35 mm cameras, by Haking Industries in Hong Kong and Chinon Industries in Japan.

Automobile and other foreign plants are welcomed in the United States for the jobs they create and the stimulus they give to the communities in which they are sited. In fact, states compete vigorously to get such plants. Thirty-three states have offices in Tokyo to extol the advantages of their states to Japanese companies contemplating plants or distribution centers in this country.

In an international trade setting dominated by multinationals operating as described above, it is small wonder that the decline of the U.S. dollar did not reduce U.S. imports and increase U.S. exports to the extent that a similar devaluation might have in an earlier day.

Many foreign manufacturers who had increased their shares of American and world markets while the dollar was overvalued were determined to hang on to those shares, even if doing so meant lower profits. Many refrained from raising their prices or tempered their price increases so that Americans would not have to use too many more of their less valuable dollars to get the yen or marks or whatever to keep on buying abroad. One analyst estimates that as the dollar's value against the yen fell, between 1985 and 1987, Japanese producers absorbed three-fourths of the impact rather than require their American customers to spend $1.85 for what $1.00 had bought.[10]

IMPACT OF THE
GLOBAL FACTORY

The option open to many foreign producers of shifting production to alternate sites significantly increased their ability to hang on to their American market shares. Some Japanese producers, in an effort to hold down costs and avoid dollar price increases, transferred some steps in the production of their products to low-cost countries. The extent of these transfers showed up in Japan's trade statistics for the mid-1980s: a 30 percent increase in imports, largely components for its products, from South Korea, Taiwan, Singapore, China, and Mexico. There was even a trickle of exports to Japan from Japanese production centers in the United States. Some Honda motorcycles from Ohio, some Sony television picture tubes from San Diego, for example. Plans to expand Japanese production facilities in the United States were expedited and continue to gain momentum.

Americans devoted to their Japanese suppliers cooperated in efforts to reduce Japanese costs. One helped his supplier make a shift to Singapore. Another, an American automobile producer whose Japanese supplier had a plant in the United States as well as in Japan, helped the Japanese company accelerate the expansion of its U.S.-based plant so its orders could be filled within this country and dollar/yen problems avoided.

STUBBORN PREFERENCES
FOR FOREIGN SUPPLIERS

One of the roadblocks that frustrated American business was the persistence with which American consumers kept on buying foreign products even as their prices rose. Of course, there was some falling off of overseas purchases, but the conviction of many American buyers that foreign products—notably foreign cars—offered better quality held import volume remarkably high.

Many American producers share American consumers' fondness for things produced by foreigners. The Commerce Department's 1987 data show that about one-third of U.S. imports were supplies and parts for U.S. plants. American multinationals, as we have seen, plan for the overseas production of many parts and components, and their imports are simply purchases by the U.S.-based corporations from their subsidiaries. Changing dollar values have no impact at all on those imports.

In addition to this in-the-family importing by multinationals, a substantial percentage of American producers buy raw materials and components abroad. Why, one might ask, is European rather than Middle Western molasses used to make citric acid in North Carolina; why are 247 parts for kitchen and bathroom faucets imported; why steel wire for radial tires? In surveys to investigate import preferences, the responses of American producer-importers repeatedly stress price and quality, price and quality.

AMERICA'S "LOST" EXPORTS

United States manufacturers explain their decisions to produce abroad on such grounds as transportation costs, the advantages of being close to the market, and the ability to give better service. They maintain that when they are near customers, they can keep track of their needs and respond to them promptly. But overseas production does have a substantial impact on the trade deficit. About half the export sales of American multinationals do not show up as U.S. exports because the orders were filled from U.S.-owned factories in other countries. Who, for example, is the largest exporter of computers from Japan? U.S. multinational IBM.

One conclusion is likely to be drawn from the capsule picture of the global village presented above: It's a difficult, complicated world out there. And it is in that difficult, complicated world that American manufacturers must become more effective competitors.

The coauthor of a best-selling book entitled *In Search of Excellence,* a survey of American companies, opens a later book with this paragraph: "There are no excellent companies. The old saw 'If it ain't broke don't fix it' needs revision. I propose: 'If it ain't broke, you just haven't looked hard enough.' Fix it anyway." [11]

There is no shortage of reports from economists, government committees, labor and business leaders, and journalists who have looked very hard indeed at American manufacturing. The chapters that follow set out what they say needs fixing and how the fixing is getting on.

CHAPTER FIVE
FRONT-OFFICE FOLLY

The front office must be the starting point for a diagnosis of manufacturing's ills, for there is fairly broad consensus on this proposition: The managers of American business must take responsibility for the sins of omission and commission that have weakened America's competitive position in the world. True, a small minority of managers and a variety of special-interest spokesmen place responsibility elsewhere: "It's all their fault." For some, "they" is the federal government, blamed at times for being overrestrictive, at times for not doing as much for U.S. business as foreign competitors' governments do. At times, "they" is "wage-gouging, uncooperative workers," at times "interest-gouging, uncooperative banks." Another favorite "they" are foreign governments that close their markets to U.S. products.

Fortunately, business leaders have been in the vanguard of those who claim that many managers in American industries did indeed "shoot themselves in the foot."

BURDENSOME
CORPORATE BUREAUCRACY

It was not a business basher but a treasury official in the Reagan administration who denounced what he terms the "corpocracy"—top management of big corporations—as "bloated, risk-averse, inefficient, and unimaginative."[12] Take "bloated" for starters. As American corporations grew by mergers and acquisitions in the 1950s and 1960s, the number of people involved in managing a growing giant multiplied: more and more divisions, departments, and sections were created; more and more head-office staff to coordinate the separated units. More and more layers of supervisors clogged the lines between top management and those who were actually turning out the product and dealing with the customers.

A bloated bureaucracy is obviously expensive in terms of salaries, benefits, and pensions. But its effects on the functioning of corporations have proved an even greater drain. Among the most harmful effects is cumbersome decision making—forty-one approvals for a price change, for example; excessively long lags between product ideas and products ready for sale. Meetings eat up the hours, paperwork engulfs desks, reports whose original purpose has long been forgotten continue to be churned out, circulated, and filed in ever expanding banks of file cabinets.

Thus, one widely employed response to the challenge of regaining competitiveness has been *restructuring*. For some corporations this involved divesting themselves of some of the companies they had acquired. For some it involved decentralizing, giving greater autonomy and responsibility to small, single-purpose units. In practically every case, becoming "lean and mean" through restructuring meant wholesale dismissals or early retirement of white-collar workers, usually at the middle-management level—a "flattening of the corporate pyramid."

Probably the best evidence that many big corporations had been absurdly overstaffed is their continued functioning after massive staff cuts. In the early 1980s wave of corporate restructuring, AT&T dropped 11,500 management positions, GM, 25,000; Ford reduced the number of white-collar workers by 30 percent and plans a further 20 percent drop. Exxon reduced its corporate headquarters' staff from 2,300 to 325. Experts maintain that reform in this area hasn't gone nearly far enough. Most companies, one expert asserts, are still oversupervised. There is no need, he argues, for more than five layers of management between the factory floor and the chief executive officer of even a giant corporation.[13]

BOTTOM-LINE MANAGERS

A second charge against American manufacturing management goes like this: It has been obsessed with quick returns and short-term earnings. This, the argument goes, has frequently meant failure to make needed long-term investments in modern plants, state-of-the-art technology, research, training programs. Investments in the future do not produce immediate returns; the bottom line on the corporation's quarterly statement does not get the lift that might result from using available funds for financial speculation in, say, the let's-buy-up-some-companies game. It is estimated that in the last few years about $500 billion that could have gone into the upgrading of manufacturing has been dissipated in paper maneuvers.

Management's defense has been that it is forced to follow this watch-the-bottom-line course by the nature of today's securities markets. Institutional investors—pension funds, insurance companies, foundations, investment companies, educational endowments, trust funds—are the major force in the securities markets. One estimate says they account for almost

90 percent, in volume and value, of the transactions on the New York Stock Exchange. These institutional investors like healthy quarterly statements. So, say corporate managers, we keep our quarterly statements looking healthy to protect the value of our stocks.

TOO FEW "DIRTY FINGERNAILS" MANAGERS

The third repeatedly cited weakness of American manufacturing management is that in recent years corporate managers have been finance and accounting people rather than production-oriented people. The nation's business schools, accused of having fostered that bias, argue that they supplied what the market wanted, and many are now giving more attention to management of production in their MBA programs.

Since it is on the production floor and on the front line of customer contact that change is most imperative, the dearth of so-called dirty-fingernails managers is probably the most serious weakness of many corporate front offices. Both the success stories of corporations that have turned themselves around and the prescriptions set forth in the how-to-regain-competitiveness literature emphasize that concern for the product, its manufacture and marketing, must be central. For too long finance people have been better paid and more likely to be on the fast track for promotion; they had the ear of top management. All this, today's experts agree, must change.

The executive secluded in his tower suite must become a corporate dinosaur. Get down on the factory floor; visit suppliers; visit dealers; listen, listen, listen, and then find new ways to *listen to customers*. These are the new ABCs of corporate management.

The company officer who says give customers my home telephone number so they can call me if they have problems; who looks for a parking space in the company lot each morning instead of sliding into a reserved slot; who can take apart a machine tool and put it together again; who sponsors the company's zero-defect-day celebration—these are the role models being offered to today's corporate managers.

CHAPTER SIX
DECLINE AND TURNAROUND IN THE AUTOMOBILE INDUSTRY

In a disquieting number of analyses of what went wrong in American manufacturing, the word *arrogant* is used to characterize corporate management in the 1960s and 1970s. And with some justification. Certainly the years of industrial dominance after World War II fortified the notion that American manufacturers were unassailable; that if they kept on doing what they were doing the United States would continue to ride the crest of the wave. The automobile industry serves well as a case study of the arrogance malady and its effects.

THE GOOD OLD DAYS

In the early years of the twentieth century, owning an automobile meant, overwhelmingly, owning a Model T Ford. The Tin Lizzie was what an automobile was supposed to be and did what an automobile was supposed to do. Then, over the years, the public's ideas changed about how a car should look and how it should feel to ride in an automobile. A whole new manufacturing technology had to be, and was, developed.

By the 1940s "automobile" meant a vehicle with a V-8 gasoline engine, automatic transmission, and rear-wheel drive. The technology to produce such a car was uniformly established throughout the industry. Nobody tried to produce an innovative automobile; competition was confined to style and dealer service; the highest profit margins went to the producers who managed their mass-production assembly lines most efficiently.

In 1955 the Big Three car producers of the United States—GM, Ford, and Chrysler—were very much interested in each other's activities but gave not a thought to the burgeoning car production in other countries. True, some Volkswagens were being bought by American customers seeking a really low priced car, but who could worry about Japanese car makers, who turned out a total of 4,000 cars that year. In fact, in 1955, cars hardly figured in world trade. Only 1.8 percent of all the cars produced worldwide were exported.

Comfortable complacency prevailed in Detroit. Descriptions of the automobile industry, well into the 1970s, are full of phrases and sentences like these: "[the automobile] was wallowing along as a conventional product"; "the constant restyling of aged chassis and drivetrains was traditional in Detroit"; "emphasis at all the American automakers had shifted away from engineering towards marketing and finance"; "I can't believe how smug those guys are. Their engineers sit in their little cubbyholes with their manuals and figure if they didn't think of it, or at least somebody in Detroit didn't think of it, it isn't worth considering."

THE INVASION BEGINS

The Japanese automobile industry in the 1960s has been described as "pitiful," groping along producing look-alike cars from British designs. By the 1970s, when Japanese penetration of the American automobile market began, the "pitiful" stage was over. The incursion began with an influx of small cars to join the other small foreign cars that had been doing well for years and did even better after the oil shocks of the 1970s.

The tale of Detroit's reaction to the small foreign-car invasion is instructive. Many efforts were made by the Big Three to produce import-fighter cars, but none were good enough to challenge the conviction of prospective small-car buyers that the foreign cars were better cars and better buys. Some maintain that Detroit could not really escape from its conviction that the vogue for small cars was some sort of aberration that U.S. customers would recover from. In fact, the charge is made that while Detroit—managed at the top by finance-oriented executives—was willing to fight little foreign cars with little U.S.-made cars, they definitely did *not* want to make a small car that was so attractive it would entice buyers away from standard-size and big cars. The profit margins on those cars were too attractive. And therein, the charge continues, lay the industry's downfall.[14]

The year 1978 was the last boom year for Detroit—9.3 million cars sold. By the early 1980s the combination of foreign competition and a severe general business recession in the United States drove the automobile industry into a real slump. Losses of over $3 billion at Ford; GM facing its first year-end loss since 1921; and the situation at Chrysler so bad that it took government-guaranteed loans to keep it alive. In 1980 the Big Three sold 6.6 million cars and lost money on those sales to the tune of $4 billion.

THE TURNAROUND BEGINS

Three years later, car sales were up only 3 percent, but those sales produced combined profits of $6 billion. Detroit had started

Auto workers leaving the General Motors assembly plant in Pontiac, Michigan, 1986, after learning that the plant was among eleven facilities in four states scheduled to be closed

to fight back, and obviously the enormous efforts to cut costs that went on during those three years brought a substantial degree of success. Every possible cost-cutting approach was used, including plant closings and massive layoffs. Ford cut its hourly work force by 45 percent; GM, by 21 percent. (Its bigger cuts came later.) Renegotiated labor contracts that permitted changes in work rules, plus updated technology, increased productivity. Shifts to offshore suppliers reduced Ford's parts production to 50 percent of its needs; GM continues to produce 70 percent of its own parts; Chrysler produces 30 percent of its parts and uses out-sourcing—purchase of parts and components from outside suppliers—for about 70 percent.

These cost-cutting programs continue to the present, supplemented by three other strategies aimed at improving the industry's competitive position: one, herculean efforts to design and produce innovative, more appealing, and more diversified models; second, a highly publicized, vigorously pursued drive to improve the quality of American cars and to change public mind-sets about their quality vis-à-vis foreign cars; third, movement toward new—Japanese-style—ways of deploying and managing workers.

Two vignettes from the how-the-automobile-industry-fought-back story warrant recounting in some detail because they are so relevant to other manufacturing industries. The first is the tale of GM's tangle with technology.[15]

THE GM STORY

Early in 1979, GM announced its intention to invest some $40 billion putting state-of-the-art technology into its production centers, a modernization program of unprecedented proportions. Almost a decade later, GM's new technology had not yet paid off. One analyst after another was asserting that the moral that must be drawn from GM's unhappy experience is this: Without changes in the way workers are trained, organized, and supervised, without changes in worker attitudes, today's sophisticated technology cannot work its potential wonders. Trouble at the GM Hamtramck, Michigan, plant—a luxury-car plant considered a showcase for high technology—was repeatedly contrasted with the situation in Fremont, California. Located there is the plant of New United Motor Manufacturing Inc. (NUMMI), a joint venture of Toyota and GM, operated under Japanese management. With far less money spent on new technology at NUMMI, the cars it produces are deemed of higher quality than those produced at any other GM plant.

The critical difference, it is agreed, is that the workers went through weeks of intensive training before production began. Japanese-style labor-management relations prevail. For example, Toyota management pledged that in a business downturn management salaries would be cut first before asking for wage concessions from union workers. In return, the union permitted reorganization of job categories from twenty-six to four broad groups, permitting a flexibility in the management of labor that increased productivity. There are no reserved parking spots for management in the company parking lot; there is no executive dining room, just a cafeteria for everybody.

THE FORD STORY

The second vignette from the automobile saga is a before-and-after story about a Ford plant in Louisville, Kentucky.[16] The Louisville plant "before" could have served as a demonstration of how not to produce automobiles: a filthy plant littered with broken and discarded parts, low worker morale evidenced by excessive absence, and bitter labor-management relations. Its output of trucks and LTDs understandably received the lowest-

American and Japanese employees work side by side at the NUMMI plant in Fremont, California. NUMMI is a joint venture of General Motors and Toyota Motor Corporation. Automobile assemblers said that working conditions were better than what they experienced under the former General Motors regime.

quality rating of any Ford plant. As orders for vehicles dropped and the night shift was laid off, rumors that shutdown was imminent seemed increasingly believable.

Then, in 1979, a new plant manager appeared on the scene. His first message to the workers pulled no punches. "Saying to hell with the company is just like saying to hell with yourself. What do you want? Do you want to make a good product, or do you want to shut down? We've got about six months left." Fortunately the new manager had two allies with whom he could work to initiate a change in plant climate. The industrial relations officer of the plant had for years been unhappy with other managers' attitudes and personnel policies. And the new head of the plant's United Auto Workers (UAW) unit was sure that the old adversarial relationship between labor and management had helped neither side.

The manager was a listener, and the gripes he heard were calls to action. The filthy plant was cleaned up and kept clean. Workers' complaint that "there's no place to sit down during our coffee breaks" produced picnic tables in convenient locations. Morale improved; quality ratings improved. Management and workers were ready for a more ambitious step.

The union knew that Ford was sponsoring—jointly with UAW—an Employee Involvement Program whose threefold goals were improving quality, productivity, and labor relations. When Louisville's application to become part of that program was accepted, an exciting possibility opened up. Ford was about to embark on production of the Ranger truck and Bronco II, a utility vehicle. Since Louisville was a truck-assembly plant, could they hope to get the new truck assigned to them and ensure themselves employment instead of shutdown?

While Ranger and Bronco II were in the design stage, drawings and models were set up in the plant, and workers were invited to comment on them. Of the 749 proposals they submitted, 542 were adopted. The Louisville plant got the Ranger assignment. Amicable negotiations between labor and management produced agreement on production processes and labor roles sharply different from the traditional automobile assembly line. Some parts of the production process were automated, with job-security clauses providing protection against layoffs associated with that automation. Production goals agreed upon for the assembly line required a speedup of the line that, in the previous climate of labor relations, would have been a strike issue.

Abandoning insistence on traditional job classifications, the union accepted the creation of a new position, "quality up grader." Three upgraders for each group of about thirty-six workers step in to help with any problem as it comes up. Empowered to pull a unit off the line or, if necessary, stop the line, they help to implement the guiding principle that "the best vehicle is the one that comes off the line right."

Louisville is a proud plant today. Absences are down; grievances handled by union officials are way down. And, according to experts, the plant is turning out quality vehicles.

Where does the automobile industry stand now? The Big Three are making money, and some automobile workers are enjoying profit-sharing checks. But nobody pretends that all is serene. As an earlier chapter made clear, the industry is very complex. The Big Three are alive and well, even if reduced to a degree to the status of merchants of foreign cars under domestic labels. But they operate in a challenging maze of foreign alliances, foreign suppliers based overseas, U.S.-based foreign suppliers, U.S.-based foreign-car producers—while looming over all of them is a worldwide overcapacity to produce cars.

Detroit's top managers today may be optimistic, pessimistic, puzzled, angry, determined, whatever. Arrogant, they are not.

CHAPTER SEVEN
SMOKESTACKS AND HIGH TECH

Most experts agree that the United States is still the world leader in technological innovation. Where Americans have fallen behind is in the incorporation of new technology into the manufacturing process. The steel industry offers an outstanding example.

TECHNOLOGY→APPLICATION LAG

The oxygen furnace was invented in 1950. Despite the fact that it was the most important technological invention in the steel industry since the turn of the century, only one small steel company made the transition to its use during the fifties. Instead, a critic of the industry reports, during that decade the industry giants were installing equipment that "was obsolete when it was built and the industry by installing it prepared itself for dying." [17] The figures on page 72 reveal how the United States lagged behind other countries in moving to the oxygen furnace and to another technological advance in steel production, con-

MODERNIZATION IN THE STEEL INDUSTRY

Percentage of Total Production
Involving Use of

	Basic Oxygen Furnace		Continous Casting	
	1960	1981	1971	1984
European Community	1.6	75.1	4.8	65.4
Japan	11.9	75.2	11.2	89.1
United States	3.4	60.6	4.8	39.6

Source: Walter Adams and James W. Brock, *The Bigness Complex: Industry, Labor and Government in the American Economy* (New York: Pantheon Books, 1986), p. 59.

tinuous casting. Small wonder that foreign competitors increased their market shares.

THE BAD DAYS

In the deindustrialization literature of the 1970s, steel was a favorite example of dying smokestack industries, and the figures on page 73 show why. They show also that the situation worsened in the eighties.

Factors other than technology→application lag figured in the industry's decline. High labor costs have unquestionably been a factor in steel companies' troubles. And a declining market for steel—more ceramics and plastics; less steel in automobiles, for example; less steel in construction—certainly made matters

IRON AND STEEL INDUSTRY

	Exports of Iron and Steel Products (millions of tons)	Imports of Iron and Steel Products (millions of tons)	Average Employment (thousands)	Net Income (billions)
1970	8.1	14.6	531	n.a.
1975	4.1	13.9	457	n.a.
1979	3.8	20.3	453	$ .8
1980	5.1	17.9	399	.7
1981	3.8	22.6	391	1.7
1982	2.6	18.8	289	−3.4
1983	1.8	19.3	243	−2.2
1984	1.7	29.5	236	×(z)
1985	1.6	27.6	208	−1.8
1986	1.5	24.2	175	−4.2

(z) Less than $50 million

n.a. Not available

Source: *Statistical abstract of the United States 1988.* U.S. Department of Commerce, Bureau of the Census, p. 722.

worse. Furthermore, the massive shift to defense expenditures that began in 1979 was substantially at the expense of expenditures on mass transportation, roads, bridges, water-treatment facilities, the nation's infrastructure. Defense spending consumes little steel compared to the enormous quantities required for the rebuilding of infrastructure.

THE ROAD BACK

The steel situation today looks brighter than it has in the recent past, but nobody says that steel's troubles are over even though steel companies' year-end reports show modest profits. The surviving members of the Big Steel group have gone through their restructuring phase. United States Steel, for example, once a superstar in American industry, is now simply a division of the conglomerate into which the original corporation was transformed, USX. National Steel is a joint venture with a Japanese producer.

Some companies have spent billions on modernization, but it is estimated that about one-third of present steel capacity is technologically obsolete. Actually, Big Steel has pared itself down so dramatically that the increased orders of early 1988 pushed production levels close to existing plants' capacity.

The industry is currently involved in efforts to promote labor-management cooperation. Using a $25,000 training grant from the Labor Department, executives from major companies in the industry joined union officials in a two-week session of training in the techniques of participation and problem solving. It was hoped that training would increase the chances for success of the so-called LMPTs (labor-management participation teams) that were being introduced in several companies. The function of LMPTs is to capitalize on steelworkers' knowledge of their jobs to increase safety and efficiency. Thus they are very similar to the quality circles—small groups of workers who gather to discuss how to improve their collective performance—which have been introduced in many other industries.

Steelworkers' reactions to the push for participation vary. With the industry in its present precarious state, they understand that cost cutting is imperative if U.S. companies are to be competitive. But, some reason, suppose their suggestions produce efficiencies that eliminate jobs. Union contracts offer protection against such a contingency, but workers worry. And there are always the cynics who simply view "participation" as a fancy term for a program to get more work out of labor.

Steel is one of the industries in which labor has moved into management roles. In return for wage concessions, the steel workers' union won substantial stock ownership, and directors nominated by the union now sit on the boards of several companies.

Steel has been helped to survive, if not helped on the road to competitiveness, by government protection. Tariffs that have been applied on imported steel since 1968 were raised in the 1980s. This help was supplemented by so-called voluntary-restraint agreements with foreign steel-exporting countries designed to limit basic steel imports to about 20 percent of the U.S. domestic market for steel. Steel wants more help, specifically with the huge pension and other costs associated with plant closings, plus assurance that the restrictions on imports will continue beyond the set expiration date in 1989.

The steel industry's basic problems persist: worldwide overcapacity to produce steel, aggressive foreign competition, and continuing inefficiency within its ranks.

LITTLE STEEL

While Big Steel was going through its times of trouble, another segment of the steel industry was thriving and continues to thrive, the so-called minimills. The minimills' formula for producing steel products that can meet foreign competitors' prices is relatively simple. Their raw material is scrap; their mills are close to markets; they use state-of-the-art technology; their nonunion labor costs are lower than Big Steel's.

Their output has been principally small wire and steel products used in making things, from basketball hoops to oil-field equipment. As the minimills move into the production of a line of steel products hitherto the exclusive domain of Big Steel—and this is expected to happen with advancing technology—pressure on the onetime giants will increase. Actually, it is generally conceded that it was competition from these U.S.-based minimills as much as foreign competition that brought disaster to Big Steel.

LAGGARDS IN
OTHER INDUSTRIES

Steel does not stand alone as a technology laggard. American tire companies knew about radial tires and did not produce them until foreign companies began producing them in the United States. Six years elapsed between the invention of the ballpoint pen and its production for the market; the videocassette recorder was invented in the United States in 1956 and never commercialized here. And there is the wonderful tale of the portable radio.

One of the earliest designs for an all-transistor miniature portable radio was developed in the mid-fifties in the corporate lab of one of the giant American companies. The link to the company's own radio business was never forged, although the circuit was licensed to a Japanese producer who incorporated it into products sold successfully in the U.S. Later, the American firm's radio business, attempting to catch up, made a photo-

copy of the Japanese circuit board as the basis for their design, only to learn to everyone's chagrin that they were copying an invention of their own lab.[18]

Could there be a better example of the communications problems in a corporate bureaucratic jungle?

THE MACHINE TOOL INDUSTRY

Probably no image of manufacturing is more familiar to the layperson than that of an assembly line, each worker on the line using a specialized piece of equipment to do his or her small task in the production of hundreds of thousands of identical products. If we are to believe the industrial prophets, that kind of assembly line mass production is not in manufacturing's future, at least not for the successfully competitive.

The industry that produces the equipment with which factory employees work is the machine tool industry, once one of the stars of the American economy. The amazing progress that industry made in the design and manufacture of machine tools explains the steady, substantial increase in productivity that characterized American manufacturing in its glory days and made possible the high wages of American manufacturing workers. In the 1960s the American machine tool industry met 96 percent of the U.S. domestic market's need and enjoyed a 23 percent share of world machine tool exports.

TROUBLE BEGINS

Machine tools are power-driven machines that cut, form, and shape metal. The traditional machine tools in which American industry excelled made parts for the widest imaginable variety of products from airplanes to vacuum cleaners, parts then put together into products on assembly lines.

In the late 1950s a partnership was formed of machine tool manufacturers, the air force, and faculty from the Massachusetts Institute of Technology with the purpose of creating a new generation of machine tools, the so-called numerically controlled (NC) machine tools. Because work for the Department of Defense was on a cost-plus basis, there was no need for the strenuous efforts to keep costs down that had produced earlier generations of increasingly productive, priced-to-the-market tools for American industry. Thus, the NC tools that emerged were expensive and complex. Those American manufacturers who wanted the sophisticated technology embodied in NC tools found that what American machine tool manufacturers were offering did not meet their needs.[19] At about the same time, the machine tool industry lost its leadership in the production of machinery for the textile industry. Massive changes in fabric production that emerged in the 1960s required changes in textile machinery that American producers did not move to provide. Machine tool manufacturers of West Germany and Japan saw the opportunity presented by these two situations and moved into the vacuum. The United States machine tool industry's slide began.

ENTER HIGH TECH

The next two giant steps in machine tool technology were also American. Computer-assisted design and computer-assisted manufacturing (CAD/CAM) came first; then, building upon CAD/CAM, came flexible manufacturing (FM) systems. The innovative nature of FM systems is suggested by this example.

One of the Big Three automakers had been buying a component for the front axle unit of one of its cars from an outside supplier. When a batch of the delivered part proved unsatisfactory, management decided to try out the FM system that it had just installed in one of its plants. Using it, company engineers were able to design and get operating, in ten weeks, tooling to produce a satisfactory axle component. The design and building of a conventional, single-purpose machine tool to turn out the desired component would have taken a year, and once built, all it would turn out would be that front axle unit. The FM system can readily be reprogrammed to become tooling for the production of other car parts.

In other words, the key to FM's importance is the word *flexible*. Admittedly enormously expensive, an FM system can meet the needs of a manufacturer operating from a backyard garage as well as those of a giant corporation's multiacre plant. It makes economically feasible production of differentiated items, in contrast to the conventional assembly line's capacity to do only mass production of identical items.

The state-of-the-art manufacturing technology just described requires a totally new contribution from labor. Failure to realize this was what caused the trouble at GM described in an earlier chapter. Manual dexterity is the prime asset on an assembly line. With the new technology, the worker must understand how it functions and be prepared to intervene when malfunction occurs.

Manufacturing involving a high tech system is an amazing sight. Deere & Company's tractor assembly plant in Waterloo, Iowa, for example, is a marvel of computer-managed production. The computer knows precisely what kind of tractor has been ordered by Dealer X in City Y. Computer control programs bring exactly the right engine, exactly the right transmission system, and exactly the right wheels together at exactly the right time. Vehicles in the process of production and the components that go into them move about the floor, under orders from the computer.[20]

POSSIBILITIES UNREALIZED

The U.S. machine tool industry today is in a sad state. By 1987 its share of the world market had dropped to 4 percent, and imports of machine tools had risen to 47 percent of the U.S. domestic market. The industry is not, for the most part, producing in American factories the sophisticated manufacturing systems that American technology created. Licensing agreements sent much production abroad, notably to Japan, and many American machine tool manufacturers are producing overseas. Joint-venture agreements have made some machine tool manufacturers salesmen for sophisticated production equipment that bears their names but was produced abroad.

In 1987 government entered the picture. In announcing the imposition of controls over machine tool imports, President Reagan stated that the revitalization of the industry "is primarily the industry's own responsibility" but that the government has a role. In addition to limits on machine tool imports from West Germany, Switzerland, Taiwan, and Japan, the Defense Department was charged to integrate the domestic industry "more fully in the defense procurement process."

BUT WHERE
ARE THE CUSTOMERS?

The machine tool industry certainly dragged its feet in putting American innovative technology into the production of modern manufacturing systems. Equally disturbing is that American manufacturers, with some notable exceptions, are not clamoring for the sophisticated production systems that could transform their factories into producers of high-quality, competitively priced, superlatively serviced products. FM technology, says one commentator, was "greeted with a yawn by U.S. manufacturers."

AN OPPORTUNITY AHEAD: SUPERCONDUCTIVITY

A new arena looms ahead in which a race is already under way to determine who will find the bridges from basic research to commercial applications to manufacturing technology. The research area is superconductivity, the development of low-resistance conductors of electricity that will function at temperatures above those that now limit the field. A recent breakthrough in this research area was described this way by a journalist:

> *The normally staid physicists at the New York meeting apparently agreed [that something big was about to happen]. Like rock music fans waiting to get into a concert, the crowd began gathering for what they dubbed the "Woodstock of physics" 2½ hours ahead of time. When the doors opened for a hastily scheduled 7:30 p.m. session on superconductivity, scientists shoved and jostled each other for the 1,150 seats. The rest craned to hear from the hallways or watched on video monitors outside. "I came to see history," declared one scientist as he elbowed his way to a seat. He wasn't disappointed. More than 50 researchers reported brand-new experimental results. Several revealed information phoned in from their laboratories just hours earlier. With only five minutes allotted to each, the session ran until 3 a.m.[21]*

Excitement over the possibilities of superconductivity has already prompted an extraordinary announcement by the president of an "eleven-point Superconductivity Initiative" designed specifically to help American business translate research into marketable technologies (Japan and the Soviet Union already have national programs on superconductivity). In announcing unprecedented steps to facilitate research, government officials were quick to stress that there had been no change in the basic position that commercial products are the responsiblity of private enterprise.

This is a story to follow.

CHAPTER EIGHT
TROUBLE
IN SILICON VALLEY

In the early 1980s, U.S. manufacturers dominated the semiconductor industry, the industry that produces the tiny silicon chips containing circuits that do calculations or store information. University- and industry-based research was reflected in the Silicon Valley plants of one new company after another, all managed by young, aggressive executives.

HIGH TECH
BROUGHT LOW

Price competition in the computer-chip industry heated up, and in an effort to reduce costs many companies moved production abroad. One proposed explanation for the industry's dramatic decline is linked to that shift. In the 1980s, the explanation goes, the market began to demand higher DRAMs (dynamic random-access memory chips), the memory chips used in computers, radar, VCRs, and everything else from missiles to talking toys. The stateside laboratories of the U.S. companies had the designs for the higher DRAMs, but the overseas factories dragged their heels in shifting production to the revised product. The Japanese also had the designs, produced what the market wanted, and virtually took over the industry.

GOVERNMENT INTERVENTION

There is general agreement that the Japanese and European rivals who knocked company after company out of business did not out-innovate the American companies. While some maintain that Japan's unfair support of its industry caused the American companies' downfall, others argue that they were beaten in a price war by rivals offering prices made possible by superior manufacturing techniques; they were beaten by chip quality that some claim is more dependable than the quality of U.S.-produced chips.

The debacle in this high-tech industry attracted wide public attention. High tech was supposed to be the wave of the future, and defense interests raised the argument that an ailing computer-chip industry threatened national security.

In September 1986, in an attempt to ameliorate price competition, Japan and the United States negotiated an agreement that included a floor price for computer chips and an understanding that American penetration of the Japanese market would be gradually increased. Shortly thereafter, the United States charged that Japan was breaking the agreement by dumping (selling below cost) chips in the United States and Southeast Asia. In retaliation, a 100 percent punitive tariff was imposed on specified Japanese electronic products.

After this move the dumping did stop, and chip prices rose, a partial explanation for the subdued optimism about the future that was voiced by industry leaders in 1987. But in the spring of 1988 industry representatives were complaining that their market share in Japan was not growing at the rate the 1986 chips agreement had seemed to promise.

AFTER THE STORM

Of the American semiconductor manufacturers who survived, only two companies produced DRAMs for the market; AT&T and IBM produce millions for themselves. Some decided to confine themselves to specialized areas of the industry in which they think they can compete successfully, producing custom-designed chips for specific purposes, for example. ASICS—application-specific integrated circuits—are used in products as diverse as automobiles, computers, and guided missiles. These chips cannot be mass-produced, and supplying them requires close, constant collaboration between customer and manufacturer. Over one hundred small companies have embarked on ASIC production, and so far there have been few failures. One of the giant companies still in the inudstry, INTEL, has a separate ASIC unit.

Some of the older chip companies that survived have teamed up with Japanese competitors. In contrast, Texas Instruments, which was once involved in a joint venture with Sony, has terminated that arrangement. It now owns four factories in Japan as well as research and production facilities in the United States, Europe, and Southeast Asia.

NOW SEMATECH

In the spring of 1987 fourteen companies in this highly competitive industry decided to try a cooperative effort against foreign competition by forming a consortium called the Semiconductor Manufacturing Technology Institute—Sematech. Their

purpose is cooperative development of advanced production techniques to take the industry into the next decade. Consortiums like Sematech were made possible by an easing of the antitrust laws that was part of the National Cooperative Research Act of 1984, and more than fifty have been organized.

Material help for Sematech came in December 1987 in the form of an appropriation of $100 million from the federal government, to be channeled through the Defense Department, which took care of half its annual budget; member companies make up the remaining half. But Sematech has already had problems. It is still in search of a chief executive and finding its members reluctant to release their top people for the job.

After some difficulty in deciding between lab research and tryout of production techniques as the organization's central mission, advanced research was the choice. But the required memorandum of understanding between Sematech and the Defense Department, spelling out exactly how Sematech is to operate, had not been finalized by the designated deadline.

SMALL IS BEAUTIFUL

The computer-chip companies that went the ASIC route to survival reflect a broad new trend in American manufacturing. In many industries, small and medium-size companies are follow-

Schematics of computer chip designs are shown here magnified hundreds of times so that IBM's Tucson, Arizona, engineers, programmers, and designers can more easily work with the intricate microscopic circuitry.

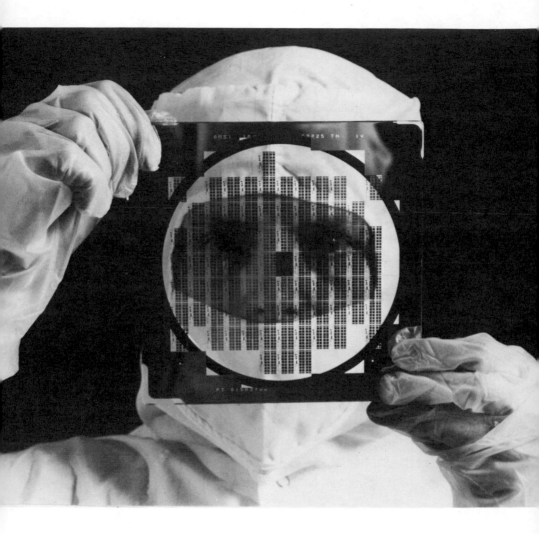

*An IBM manufacturing technician holds up a glass mask
containing images of the company's four-million-bit
memory chip at the IBM semiconductor manufacturing
and development facility in Essex Junction, Vermont.
IBM and AT&T are contributing hundreds of millions
of dollars' worth of computer chip technology to the
cooperative research group known as Sematech.*

ing the how-to-be-competitive advice that is coming from a number of business analysts and economists. It goes like this: Create your own niche in a broad market and produce a high value-added product for that market. A high value-added product is one characterized by innovative design based on specifically identified customer requirements; it is a product of superior quality; along with the product go exceptional service and exceptional response to customers' problems or requests.

These niche producers are finding that ordinary products, customized and produced with extraordinary efficiency, by labor flexible enough to do almost any production job, can be sold in the U.S. domestic market and in overseas markets in the face of foreign competition. The 80 employees of LDI Manufacturing are turning out exhaust fans tailored to serve Pizza Hut, Kentucky Fried Chicken, White Castle, and Taco Bell, plus other ventilating, heating, and air-conditioning systems. They install, inspect, and train the customers' employees in the use of their products. In one of Ritron's two plants, 140 employees turn out two-way radios that compete successfully with Motorola and Japanese competitors.[22]

Even big companies may begin to think small. A major company in the chemical industry has reduced emphasis on the production of basic chemicals for an undifferentiated market and turned instead to the production of specialty chemicals for the needs of smaller, narrower markets.

Companies with fewer than 250 employees account for 42 percent of today's manufacturing jobs. Some predict that that percentage could rise to more than half in the 1990s. Right now, the feisty little niche companies are winning respect as leaders in the revitalization of American manufacturing.

CHAPTER NINE
QUALITY AND OTHER PROBLEMS

A critical look at quality in American manufacturing must be prefaced with recognition that some products of some U.S. industries are better than comparable products made by anyone anywhere. A partial list of examples would include products as diverse as satellites, fly-fishing rods, stereo speakers, cotton percale bed sheets, and computer work stations. Their status as top of the line is recognized worldwide. That said, a broader and less rosy picture must be recorded.

THE QUALITY PROBLEM

The problem of product quality came up in the automobile industry. It came up in the semiconductor industry. It comes up in any treatment of U.S. manufacturing because, as one industry analyst puts it, "At some point in its middle industrial history, perhaps around 1960, America began the long descent in the quality of its manufactured goods. It was hardly an overnight transformation, but there was a period in which the rush to exploit the quickening demand for consumer goods swept aside pride-of-workmanship in the name of quick profit."[23] A disturbing indictment, for quality is generally accepted today as "the crux of global competitiveness."

"Churn out work as fast as you can and reject the worst 5 percent of what emerges." Such a directive falls far short of a formula for quality production, but industry critics deem it typical of standards that prevailed for far too long in far too many American industries. Quality control under that standard meant simply inspection plus rejection of the worst.

The importance of product quality in the struggle to hold on to or build market share can hardly be overemphasized. Car recalls, for example, to fix defective parts or potentially dangerous performance had a devastating effect on American automobile sales in the early 1980s.

The drive to increase American manufacturing competitiveness has produced a wave of interest in quality, but unfortunately many quality campaigns have been ill conceived. Instead of initiating programs to get work right in the first place, efforts have focused on more rigorous inspection of finished work. For some companies the results have been disastrous. More defects are found, and the costs of fixing them have raised costs of production to a degree that threatens the basic purpose of the whole enterprise, becoming more competitive.

The quality circles mentioned above have burgeoned in American factories, but many have had no real impact on performance. Inadequate training in preparation, hostility of line supervisors, lack of follow-through on suggestions, absence of a genuine commitment on the part of top management to a philosophy of worker participation—any one of these can limit the usefulness of these potentially creative group meetings.

When programs to achieve competitive excellence include giving workers both responsibility and authority in the management of their tasks, success stories do emerge. For example, at one company, workers involved in the production of water pumps were given the opportunity to become genuinely involved in planning and evaluating their work. They increased their productivity 300 percent, reduced waste in utilization of materials, and produced a better pump. On an automobile assembly line, one out of every sixty cars required rework of the fit of hoods or bumpers. When workers were given the opportunity to restructure the process of fitting the metal to the frame, the ratio dropped dramatically.

A final, painfully instructive story from the automobile industry. Dr. W. Edward Deming is a distinguished American statistician. Back in the 1950s nobody in Detroit was interested in his proposals for statistical quality control. The Japanese, struggling through the infancy of their automobile industry, welcomed his ideas and used them in their plants. The results are history, and Dr. Deming has been a widely respected figure in Japan for years. Now in his eighties, he recently accepted the invitation of an American car company to serve as a quality consultant.

MARKETING AT HOME

A basic weakness of U.S. manufacturers as marketers, it is charged, has been their failure to exploit opportunities. Too few companies have taken advantage of the competitive edge inherent in being in and part of the world's largest market, the $4 trillion economy of the United States. A few outstanding companies, by using the communications technology now available, have shown that links among suppliers, factories, distribution centers, and retailers make possible a whole new level of speedy response to customers' needs—an enormous competitive advantage. Here are two such success stories.

Some foreign manufacturers can produce a man's shirt and get it to the United States for a total cost that is one-third of a domestic manufacturer's cost of producing the same product. The U.S. textile and apparel manufacturers who have been able to survive that kind of competition—and some have—have taken the basic step of introducing state-of-the-art technology in their plants. Then they have established sophisticated communications networks among textile mills, truckers, apparel producers, and customers. Fabric from domestic mills can thus reach customers in one-third the time needed to get fabric from Taiwan; the interval between design of product and delivery of product has been cut in half. Taking full advantage of the fact that they are here, the market is here, and Taiwan is way out there, those U.S. manufacturers have survived with a formula of aggressive marketing plus speedy delivery plus top-flight service.

MARKETING ABROAD

"It's been amazing to see the change in attitude among American businesses. They are starting to understand that the falling dollar is a window of opportunity and now is the time to strike."[24] *Change* is the key word in that 1987 comment by a Commerce Department official. According to the department's estimates, 80 percent of U.S. manufactured exports are produced by only 250 companies. The vast majority of small and midsized businesses have not been involved in international trade. In fact, they have been dubbed "insular laggards" because of their unwillingness to make the leap into unknown, "strange" foreign places. "To most small or medium-sized companies in the Middle West," the Commerce official observed, "California is an export market."

A number of reasons are offered to explain U.S. manufacturers' reluctance to storm overseas markets. For one thing, many of them have been unable or unwilling to respond appropriately to the unfamiliar behavior of overseas customers. Patience seems

An example of the successful exportation of U.S. culture, the fast-food company McDonald's came to Japan in 1971 in a fifty-fifty joint venture with a Japanese company.

necessary. Lengthy negotiations are often needed, particularly if the customer is a foreign government. A small company may try to break into a foreign market by exhibiting its product in an international trade show. The exhibit attracts much favorable attention; dozens of inquiries come in from potential buyers; then silence. Companies that give up at that point are out of the picture. Those that are willing to invest six to nine months on the follow-up efforts that the potential foreign customers expect may get orders.

Some find it difficult to live with the bill-paying habits of European and other foreign customers. Comfortable with the U.S. practice of a six- to eight-week interval between billing and payment, they find disturbing foreign customers' assumption that a three- to nine-month interval is acceptable.

The American commitment to yards and pounds has made an industrial world that has gone metric just too much trouble for some companies to cope with. And take the matter of learning foreign languages. Over a thousand subsidiaries of U.S. firms are operating in Japan. In their offices, during the business day, Americans can function with English only. But contact with wholesalers is very important, and fewer than 1 percent of Japanese wholesalers speak English. Furthermore, any after-hours contacts, essential for establishing relationships, require ability to speak Japanese. Yet nearly 90 percent of U.S. executives in Japan don't learn the language.

In contrast, consider the Oregon lumberman who began his campaign to sell finished lumber to Japanese construction firms by traveling all over Japan. Not only did he seek out potential customers; he visited plants of Japanese lumber suppliers who would be his competitors. He arranged for the foremen in his plant to be instructed in Japanese ways of grading lumber. And to prepare for the visit of some likely Japanese customers, he built a Japanese-style teahouse in which to entertain them. He now enjoys substantial business relationships in Japan.

Many U.S. manufacturers have been unwilling to adapt their products to foreign tastes. Huge refrigerators for tiny Japanese kitchens, blond, blue-eyed dolls for African markets, clothing that doesn't fit "un-American" body types—these are familiar examples. Far more serious for the company involved were the marketing errors made by a major manufacturer of personal computers. It was the first American company to sell them in Japan. But it failed to offer a machine that could process the characters in which Japanese is written; it did not provide an instruction manual written in Japanese.

Successes, where adaptation to foreign markets has been made, are impressive. To sell its NC manufacturing system in Western Europe, GE developed a system that could use both metric and English measurement systems. Because the voltage of the electrical systems differs from country to country in Europe, the system was designed to be operable with varying voltage.

The Japanese like squid, so Pizza Hut offers pizza with squid topping; Koreans don't like salt, so salt-free topping is available; a doughnut adapted to the Japanese less sweet-loving taste did wonders for Mister Donut's sales.

Eastman Kodak offers an instructive example of product differentiation to meet the requirements of a foreign market. Darkrooms are few and far between in Japan, so it is easy to understand why Japanese professional photographers were enthusiastic customers for film that can be processed in normal room light.

SERVICE

Another frequently cited weakness of American manufacturers as marketers is their failure to offer competitive levels of service after making sales. On the consumer level, for example, an

American who lived in Tokyo for many years reports on his happy experience with a Japanese washing machine. Recounting a prompt, courteous, free service call, he observed that "the Japanese take for granted follow-up service that would make a typical American manufacturer choke." [25]

On the production level, stories like this recur. An American car manufacturer placed two orders for machine tools, one with a Tokyo firm, one with an established U.S. machine tool firm. When the Tokyo equipment arrived, two Tokyo engineers arrived with it. The machine tool was operating smoothly in two weeks with all the snags of the start-up period taken care of. In contrast, it took eight of the car manufacturer's own engineers several months to get the American equipment to a satisfactory operating level. No help came on the initiative of the vendor.

There are repeated complaints of U.S. manufacturers who fail to pay attention to customers' problems and reactions, sometimes with disastrous results. Consider the giant computer company that didn't really listen when customers repeatedly told its representatives: We can't use your new product with that other unit we bought from you last year. Other companies, responsive to this problem of incompatibility, turned their R & D efforts to solving it and almost toppled the giant with their sales of network systems.

LABOR MISMANAGEMENT

Perhaps the most serious general weakness in American manufacturing can be seen in a comparison of American and Japanese ways of organizing and supervising labor on the factory floor. For example, a visitor to a Japanese assembly plant tells of finding it surprisingly similar to an American plant until trouble with a machine shut the line down. In an American plant,

A Japanese-style approach to labor is used at this Nissan plant in Smyrna, Tennessee, and is credited with increased production and worker loyalty.

the visitor knew, foremen and workers would dicker over the job classifications from which help should be drawn to find the problem and fix it. The big concern would be to ensure respect for everyone's exclusive job turf. On the Japanese line, the operator of the machine that was down immediately began efforts, with the foreman's help, to get the machine going again. Other workers pitched in to get the halted work in progress ready for start-up.

Every prescription for change in American management of the manufacturing process emphasizes the need for change in labor/management perceptions of each other, their roles on the factory floor, and their relationships in routine contacts and at the bargaining table. A major barrier to productivity growth, analysts say, has been management's failure to look upon its labor force as an invaluable asset, to involve its workers in every aspect of the productive process, from design to final inspection, to invest heavily in their training, to give them responsibility, to motivate productive performance with substantial financial incentives. On the other hand, analysts maintain that American labor has been unduly insistent upon rigid job classifications and strict adherence to work rules; has expected and seemed comfortable in an adversarial relationship with management.

Today it is argued that changes in manufacturing technology and the intensity of competition are making the management posture just described too costly to maintain. The argument goes like this: In an earlier day, improvements in manufacturing technology generally meant smaller steps in the production process, simpler, narrower jobs, and a faster production pace. That day is over. Improved technology today is more likely to involve the installation of sophisticated systems such as those described in an earlier chapter—NC machine tools, CAD/CAM, FM systems. These technologies, to be maximally effective, demand totally changed roles for labor.

Many American manufacturers are moving toward more productive use of labor. The work team concept is being increasingly introduced. Among the companies that have adopted it in varying degrees are Procter & Gamble, Cummins Engine, GM, GE, Westinghouse, IBM, Xerox, and Polaroid. In a team setting, the team as a whole is responsible for a specific segment of the production process, perhaps the installation of all the accessories on an engine; the team decides how it will do its joint task. Frequently, all team members can do all the jobs within the joint task and can rotate them. The team evaluates its work before passing it along to the next production unit. For example, in the furniture-production unit of a major corporation in which 65 percent of the work force are members of teams working with state-of-the-art technology, the plant can shift smoothly from the production of one special order to another; workers consult with customers; customers visit the plant to see their work in progress.

Critics of American manufacturers maintain that many are misusing automation, viewing it "as a tool to reduce the need for labor, not as a tool to aid labor in adding value to the product." Many of the reported failures with robots, it is claimed, stem from management's failure to integrate them appropriately as an aid rather than a replacement for labor.

More serious is this assertion from critics: When manufacturers, in an effort to cut costs, send production to low-labor-cost sites offshore or across the border, they put their future in jeopardy. To lose close contact with and total control of production by farming it out means losing control of quality, losing the capacity for quick response to customers' needs, losing the initiative for innovation that can come from the factory floor when involved workers are teamed with management aware of their potential.

Hard times have in many instances forced into being unprecedented levels of cooperation between American labor and

management: concessions on wages, job classifications, and work rules from labor; job security and profit-sharing commitments from management. But overall, the adversarial relationship between labor and management that has characterized American industrial history persists. An unfortunate state of affairs and an acknowledged barrier to effective competing.

Many American manufacturers have worked and are working to ensure that the weaknesses recited above are eradicated from their operations. Some have had noteworthy success. But it is American business leaders, not business bashers, who continue to say that "we have a long way to go."

This is the Ford Motor Company's largest facility, the Rouge Plant in Detroit, Michigan. In a new contract negotiated between Ford and the United Auto Workers in 1982, labor swapped wage and benefit concessions for job security and profit-sharing provisions.

CHAPTER TEN
HOW IS LABOR FARING?

I want the people in a team to be able to go home at night and really say, "I built that car." That is my dream.

Pehr Gyllenhammar, chairman
of the board, Volvo Corporation

For labor, the drive to restore competitiveness to American manufacturing has had an up side and a down side. The up side, as the previous chapter suggested, is emerging acceptance of new perceptions of labor, perceptions that underlie the Volvo chairman's dream: Workers are a company's most valuable resource; their responsible involvement in the production process, their pride in their work, are central to a company's success.

GIVEBACKS, TRADE-OFFS, CHOICES

The down side of the drive for competitiveness is aptly summarized in the observation that "foreign competition continues to discipline labor markets."

105

The newspaper story of a recent labor negotiation between the motor division of a major conglomerate and the workers in its nine motor plants began this way: "It is a story that could be told about any one of a hundred gritty, old American manufacturing businesses struggling to compete in the 1990s. It is a story about bitter choices." [26] The choice for the motor division workers was to take a pay cut or have no job. The background went like this. First came shrinkage of the U.S. domestic market for motors from $3 billion to $2 billion, as foreign products entered the country—air conditioners, for example— with motors produced abroad already installed in them. Next came a price war between the conglomerate and its U.S. competitors, a war that drove earnings down to a level the conglomerate deemed unacceptable. So its position when negotiations began was firm: Unless workers accepted a two-dollar hourly wage cut, it would be forced to "shrink, close, or sell" its motor division.

The 1,250 workers to whom this ultimatum was delivered had seen about 5,000 workers in the motor division lose their jobs as the company closed other plants and moved work offshore to its plants in Singapore and Mexico. At those offshore sites, base hourly wages at the time were $1.49 and 79¢, respectively; the base hourly wage in the U.S. plant was $10.92. Because there had been no new hires for years, the length of service of those 1,250 workers averaged 23 years. Retirement benefits loomed large in their thinking.

Negotiations that stretched over a period of months finally produced a contract that included (1) a reduction of $1.20 in the base hourly wage, (2) a guarantee of job security for present workers but with an escape hatch from that guarantee if motor orders declined, and (3) promises by the company to pay modest bonuses when profits increased; to restore cost-of-living raises in 1991; to invest $200 million in modernizing the motor division's plants. Clearly the workers had received some trade-offs for the $1.20 giveback. They voted 2 to 1 to accept the contract.

Similar trade-offs were involved in an electronics industry negotiation, with the bargaining process enlivened by one colorful episode. When workers were asked to accept fairly substantial cuts in wages and benefits and the union said no, company negotiators took a group of union officials to its plant in Mexico. This plant, the union people were assured, can do exactly what you do in Ohio. If we do not get from you the concessions we have asked for, we will be forced to move production here. The concessions were made.

In the contract reached by United Steelworkers of America after a strike against USX, labor traded a wage cut, adjustment of vacation and holiday time, and changes in health insurance for a profit-sharing plan and two interesting forms of job protection. First, the company agreed to limit the practice of contracting out work to nonunion shops, thus preventing some layoffs. Second, the union agreed to dismissal of 1,346 workers in return for the company's promise that it would offer pensions to two older workers for each of the 1,346 let go. The hope was that retirements would create job openings to which laid-off workers could be recalled.

In another contract, averting a plant closing involved union agreement to a wage freeze and acceptance of a three-tier wage system. Instead of the $8.00–$14.70 an hour scale for then current workers, workers recalled from layoff were to be paid $3 per hour less; new hires, $5 less. The differentials were to be phased out within five to seven years. Two-tier wage systems have been a popular cost-cutting device. But some companies that have tried them have found they created so much tension between lower-paid and higher-paid workers that they have either given up the system or speeded up the phaseout stage.

When the UAW began negotiations with Ford in the fall of

1987, everyone in the automobile industry knew that job security was to be the paramount issue, and whatever pattern was set with Ford would figure in negotiations ahead with Chrysler and GM. What emerged was a ground-breaking contract for the industry: job protection for workers, hedged with a degree of protection for the company. The contract guaranteed, for its three-year life, the jobs of the 104,000 factory workers then employed by Ford. The guarantee will not hold if car sales decline or if the cost of maintaining employment of excess workers exceeds $500 million. To permit a shrinkage of the work force by attrition—nonreplacement of workers who leave the company voluntarily—the contract provides that the number in the guaranteed work force may be cut by one for every two workers who leave. Thus, if 1,000 workers retired, the guaranteed work force would drop from 104,000 to 103,500. Workers agreed to cooperate in getting rid of work rules that hampered productivity and accepted in principle the work-team production model as opposed to the conventional assembly line.

Some final points about current trends in compensation systems for manufacturing workers: First, the number of COLA (cost-of-living adjustment) clauses in labor contracts has been declining steadily. Second, profit sharing and other forms of incentive pay are increasingly used, and while the payout profit level that triggers such plans is not always reached, some substantial distributions have been reported. In 1987, for example, Ford hourly workers received checks averaging $2,100 under their profit-sharing plan.

Since union contracts set the terms of employment for so many manufacturing workers, a final question must be raised: What can be said of the state of unions in U.S. manufacturing today? As of 1987, about 23 percent of manufacturing workers belong to unions. Union workers still earn about one-third more than nonunion, but the latter group has seen greater increases since 1982.

Strikes are down significantly. Between 1945 and 1980, two

to four hundred strikes occurred each year; there were only fifty-two work stoppages in 1985. And companies' reactions to strikes have changed markedly. Hiring of replacements for striking workers, generally not done during the 1950s through the 1970s, is now fairly general practice, and replacement workers cross picket lines. Management's posture is, increasingly, "We are going to tough it out," an attitude consistent with the general appraisal of today's employers made by one labor lawyer: "not brass-knuckled, but people who are sharp-penciled." [27]

TODAY'S NEW JOBS

Turn now to the workers who lost their jobs in manufacturing because of foreign competition or as the result of American companies' efforts to become leaner and more competitive. Some became part of a group classified as "discouraged workers." Estimated by the Labor Department to number about three million individuals, these are people who want to work but are not looking for work. Some have given up trying to find jobs because they don't believe jobs are available. Some are former factory workers who are not willing to take jobs that pay less than they had been getting. The "discouraged" group does not show up in unemployment percentages. Only persons without jobs who are actively looking for work are counted as unemployed.

What kind of jobs were available for those displaced factory workers who did seek work? Where will the jobs be for new entrants to the labor market? The number of people at work in the United States has increased fairly steadily from 1982 on and that trend is projected to continue. As of 1987, over thirteen million new jobs had been created since 1979; on that point there is no disagreement. There is, however, substantial controversy over the quality of these jobs.

A pioneer study on this subject compared the wage levels

of the jobs created during the 1979–85 period and two earlier periods. Because real average annual wage (money wages adjusted for inflation) reached their post–World War II peak in 1973, the directors of the study chose the median wage for that year, $14,800, as their base for comparisons. The *median wage* is the wage in the middle of the whole range of wages paid. In other words, in 1973 half the nation's workers received less than $14,800 per year; half earned more. The study established three categories of jobs: *low-wage,* jobs paying less than half the 1973 median (below $7,400); *mid-wage,* jobs paying between $7,400 and $29,600; *high-wage,* jobs paying more than twice the 1973 median wage (above $29,600). The graph on page 111 shows the three-period comparison.

Comparing wages in three different periods is tricky because prices change over the years. So the new-job wages for each period were all "translated" into dollars of the same purchasing power. (Computers do this with the greatest ease.) For the graph on page 111 all the new-job wages were translated into dollars with 1986 purchasing power before the percentages were computed. That's why the graph says the wages are "in constant 1986 dollars."

IMPACT OF
PART-TIME WORK

Two explanations are offered for the recent dramatic surge of low-wage jobs. First, the expansion of part-time jobs, that is, jobs offering fewer than thirty-five hours of work per week. Just under 30 percent of the new jobs created between 1979 and 1985 fell into the part-time category. This percentage acquires new significance when combined with the finding that a substantial percentage of the individuals who took part-time jobs had been looking for full-time jobs. The second explanation has

THE NEW JOBS ARE PAYING LESS

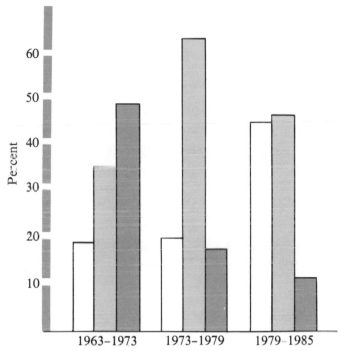

Percentages of new jobs in high-, middle- and low-wage positions; wages are in constant 1986 dollars.

☐ Low Wage: Less than $7,400/year

▨ Mid-Wage: $7,400–$29,600/year

▪ High-Wage: More than $29,600/year

Source: Barry Bluestone and Bennett Harrison, "The Grim Truth About the Job 'Miracle'," *New York Times,* February 1, 1987, Sec. 3, p. 3.

already appeared in another context: the decline, between 1979 and 1985, of the number of jobs in the higher-paying manufacturing industries and the rising number of jobs in the lower-wage non-goods-producing (service) sector.

This pioneer study's conclusions have been frequently challenged, but later figures confirm its basic finding: The preponderance of jobs currently being created are in the lower-pay categories. For example, 1986 saw 2.4 million jobs added to the economy. Sixty-seven percent were in these two categories: retail sales; health and general business services. As of March 1987 the average weekly wage in retail sales was $174; in health and general business services, $270; in manufacturing, $407.

A further indication of the lower quality of many service-sector jobs is a comparison of manufacturing versus service-sector pension benefits. A study made early in the 1980s found 86 percent of manufacturing workers covered by pension plans and only 48 percent of the workers in service jobs so protected.[28]

Clearly there is a link between growing ranks of part-time workers and cost cutting to increase competitiveness. Part-time jobs are mostly in sales, nonprofessional services, clerical work, or unskilled labor. Their median wage is $4.42 compared to the $7.43 median for full-time workers. Furthermore, health insurance, pension plans, life insurance, paid sick days, paid vacations—all these benefits are exceptions rather than the rule for part-time workers. As of early 1988 almost 30 million workers were part-timers. It is estimated that about one-quarter of that total want full-time work and that perhaps as many as half of those entering recently created part-time jobs want full-time work.

TEMPORARY WORKERS

Of the 13.5 million jobs created during the six years of recovery from the 1981–82 recession, between one and three million are filled by temporary, full-time workers. They are not tracked separately by the Labor Department but merged with permanent workers in the nation's employment statistics as "employed."

The same motivation that explains increased use of part-time workers operates here: to achieve lower labor costs. Furthermore, "temps" make it easy to adjust the work force to business conditions. A third reason for the escalating number of temps has been identified. Small companies (those with fewer than one or two hundred workers) have traditionally been the relatively heavy users of temporary workers, and it is small and medium-size companies—not the corporate giants—that have produced the new jobs of the 1980s.

Like part-time employees, temps are not included in a company's benefits program. So for both temps and part-timers the argument is advanced that government, at taxpayers' expense, will have to provide the safety nets that company insurance and benefit plans provide for the nation's full-time employees.

THE BIG PICTURE

In terms of earnings, the big picture for manufacturing workers and for American labor in general is not promising. So far as manufacturing workers are concerned, increases in productivity, averaging 4 percent in recent years, have not been matched by increases in manufacturing wages. During the same years, hourly compensation of American factory workers, adjusted for inflation, rose an average of eight-tenths of 1 percent. The increased earnings that have flowed from productivity increases have in some cases gone into capital investment; in others, they have made competitive price cuts possible. In some instances the gains have simply been absorbed as profits.

And these figures, unpleasant as they are, are relevant to the future course of manufacturing wages in the United States and very relevant to America's ability to compete in the global village. In 1987 the average total compensation (wages plus benefits) of U.S. factory workers was $13.09 an hour. Japan's average is lower but moving up. Comparable figures for Western Europe are as good or better than the U.S. average. But six other countries of the world—South Korea, Brazil, Mexico, Hong Kong, Taiwan, and Singapore—have modern factories that can turn out many products comparable to U.S. products. And each of these six countries has an average hourly wage below $3.00 an hour. Superior American productivity does indeed warrant a differential over the six low-wage competitors. Nonetheless, unless wages *there* move up, continued and more severe downward pressure on manufacturing wage levels *here* is inevitable.

As for labor in general, median family income measured in constant 1985 dollars was $29,172 in 1973; it was $27,735 in 1985, $28,902 in 1986. As explained on page 110, "constant 1985 dollars" means you can forget about inflation; the figures have been adjusted to make comparisons legitimate. And the comparisons are disquieting. More of us are working, but we are not as well off as we were fifteen years ago.

How is labor faring? Well, there is an up side and a down side.

CHAPTER ELEVEN
WHAT ROLE FOR GOVERNMENT?

"We must level the playing field." That slogan, which loomed large in the rhetoric of the 1988 presidential campaign, compresses into an attractively familiar idiom this line of argument:

- A major barrier to the ability of U.S. manufacturers to compete in the global marketplace are the industrial policies pursued by the governments of our major industrial rivals, the countries of Western Europe and Japan.

- These industrial policies encompass assistance to business that far exceeds that which business receives from the U.S. government.

- Thus, these industrial policies make the global marketplace an unfair arena of competition.

- Therefore, the U.S. government should act to make the arena of international trade competition more equitable for American players.

115

Most of the emphasis in this book has been on improving the skills of the American players rather than improving the conditions under which they play, but the playing-field argument is persuasive. So, as background for considering what the U.S. government's role should be in the drive to regain American competitiveness, it seems essential to take a look at exactly what it is "they" do in pursuit of their industrial policies that creates an unfair playing field.

THEIR WAY—INDUSTRIAL POLICY

Industrial policies have been defined as "measures used by governments to restructure, strengthen, or promote specific domestic industries." Or, another phrasing: "The essence of industrial policy is the selective intervention of government in the economy because the market is not giving rise to what is judged to be an acceptable industrial outcome." [29]

Among the developed nations of the world, France, West Germany, Sweden, Canada, and Japan have industrial policies; in the "newly industrializing countries" group, Mexico, Brazil, South Korea, and India have industrial policies. While the United States does not have an industrial policy, it does employ many of the protective and restrictive practices that industrial policy nations use to achieve their objectives.

Japan gets the most attention when industrial policy is discussed, but it was not the originator of the practice. Oddly enough, we got the ball rolling. As a condition for receiving aid under the Marshall Plan, participating nations had to draw up a plan that showed how the aid would be used. In France, the Planning Commission established to perform that Marshall Plan task is the same commission that manages French industrial policy today.

It gathers information about the country's industries and on the basis of that information targets industries to be helped. It decides how state-of-the-art technology can be brought to the targeted industries and how they can become more competitive in international markets. The commission's recommendations to those ends are not mandatory upon the companies involved, but the government does have a wide range of inducements at its disposal. It can offer tax benefits; give research and development grants; make loans at preferential interest rates. With this kind of help, why shouldn't companies in the targeted industries undertake investment projects consistent with the government's goals?

In the mid-1960s, West Germany followed France into the practice of formulating and implementing industrial policy. Government, unions, and employers' associations take part in a consultation process that is less formal and public than the comparable process in France. The sectors of the economy targeted for promotion or reduction are not announced as they are in France.

The techniques used to achieve industrial policy goals are much the same in all the countries involved—"inducements" such as those mentioned above and others that will emerge in what follows—but creative wrinkles appear. For example, a loan made by the West German Venture Financing Corporation, part of West Germany's industrial policy machinery, need not be repaid unless the investment for which the loan was sought brings the hoped-for results in increased productivity or competitiveness.

When Japan embarked upon industrial policy, it significantly broadened the scope of government activism. In fact, the term Japan Inc. is frequently used in referring to Japanese business, the implication being that the nation and the nation's business firms are one entity. That, of course, is not the case. The Japanese Ministry of International Trade and Industry (MITI) exercises a wide range of control over Japanese business, but

Japanese companies can and at times do act contrary to MITI's recommendations or requests. This is the kind of action MITI can take. During the years when Japan was targeting the machine tool industry for development, a company that had a very low share of the market in a particular machine tool line was required to stop producing that line and to concentrate on other lines. Advances in technology had to be shared within the industry. There are specific procedures for working with industries officially designated as "depressed." Labor unions have a voice in decisions about scrapping or mothballing excess productive capacity.

EXAMPLES OF INDUSTRIAL POLICY IMPACT ON U.S. MANUFACTURERS

During the early years of its post–World War II industrial development, Japan placed high tariffs on all products that would compete with Japan's then-infant industries. This completely shut U.S. producers out of the Japanese market. Although over the years these tariff walls have come down to an average rate as low as the U.S. tariff average, U.S. manufacturers maintain that other, more subtle barriers, such as rigid inspection procedures, deprive them of opportunities to do business in Japan. Not just manufacturers complain. The American construction industry has been trying for years to be allowed to bid on Japanese construction projects; U.S. farmers protest that they are prevented from competing with Japan's far less efficient producers.

The strict import licensing system of Brazil protects the state-owned enterprise that controls 60 percent of Brazil's steel output; no steel product that is produced in Brazil may be imported. When that country decided to develop its small computer industry, it closed the door to imports. Brazilians had to pay five to ten times prevailing world prices for their personal computers, but the industry did indeed thrive.

For an example of more sophisticated industrial policy techniques, take the case of large-scale generating and transmission equipment. This is the equipment with which power companies produce electric power and get it to their customers. The countries of Western Europe and Japan produce it, as does the United States. European and Japanese companies buying this equipment must buy from their home producers; U.S. companies are almost totally excluded from those markets. But they are also at a disadvantage in other markets because of the two-tier price system that prevails in Western Europe and Japan. Here's how it works: A European company, buying from a producer in its own country, pays one price for a generator. A Korean company, inquiring about the same generator from the same company, is quoted a lower price. That low price, made possible by the higher price paid by domestic buyers, obviously makes the European generator very attractive to the Korean buyer. The U.S. producer competing for the Korean sale may not be able to meet that low price and loses the sale.

SHOULD WE FOLLOW "THEM" INTO INDUSTRIAL POLICY?

If this is what industrial policy is and these are the kinds of moves typical of its implementation, should the United States fight fire with fire, formulate and implement an industrial policy of its own? In the early deindustrialization-talk days, some affirmative answers to that question were voiced. But today there is virtually complete consensus that the basic thrust of industrial policy, the central planning, the targeting of industries for growth or industrial euthanasia, is not "the American way." Consensus does seem to be developing in favor of a more aggressive, assertive posture for the U.S. government on international trade matters, but not for central planning and targeting. Legislation to authorize an industrial-policy planning process in the interests of American competitiveness would be politically impossible.

WHAT ROLE FOR THE GOVERNMENT, OUR WAY?

Then what role should the government play in the drive to restore American competitiveness? There follow some proposals that, in one quarter or another, have been offered to define what the U.S. government should do. As background and viewpoints emerge on each proposal, readers might consider where they stand and arrive at their own formulations of an appropriate government agenda.

EXISTING TRADE LAWS SHOULD BE BOTH STRENGTHENED AND VIGOROUSLY ENFORCED.

Present law provides remedies for two specific unfair trade practices, dumping and subsidies. When American producers in an industry complain to the Commerce Department that Country A is dumping Product X, the U.S. International Trade Commission (ITC) investigates. If it certifies that (1) dumping is going on and (2) American producers are being hurt, an anti-dumping duty is placed on X that makes it much more difficult for the foreign producer to continue selling X at an unfairly low price.

In recent months some companies have been filing, under the dumping clause, complaints that foreign competitors are not passing through to their dollar prices the full effect of the dollar's lowered value. The foreign producers, they claim, are selling their products at less than their fair value. For example, acting on a complaint filed by an American producer of roller bearings, which are widely used in transportation equipment, ITC investigators found that despite the fall in the dollar's value against the yen, which should have raised dollar prices for the bearings, no price rise at all had occurred between March 1 and August 31, 1986. The Japanese firms had decided to take a loss rather than sacrifice market share.

It is too early to predict whether dumping complaints on the basis just cited will result in punitive action. But, in general, American producers are satisfied with current enforcement of the dumping clause.

Suppose a foreign company is able to undersell American producers because that foreign company's government is paying it a *subsidy* for every product it exports. When U.S. trade officials determine that this is going on and that American producers are being hurt by the subsidies, a remedy similar to the antidumping duty is used, a countervailing duty equal to the foreign government's subsidy. This, of course, wipes out the advantage the subsidy had created and protects American producers. It is generally agreed that this clause of trade law is being effectively enforced.

Specific suggestions for strengthening existing trade law focus on bringing it up to date to deal with today's competitive tactics and to reduce the range of presidential discretion in enforcing the law. For example, it is proposed that *targeting,* like dumping and subsidies, should be specifically designated an unfair trade practice and a specific penalty prescribed. In other words, if a competitor nation targets a specific industry for export growth in order to capture a larger world-market share, that act, by definition, should be an unfair trade practice, and a punitive response should be imposed.

On the matter of presidential discretion, this is the line of argument: Section 301 of the basic Trade Act of 1974 as amended says:

> *The President is authorized to take all appropriate action, including retaliation, to obtain removal of any act, policy, or practice of a foreign government which is found to . . . be unjustifiable, unreasonable, or discriminatory and which burdens or restricts U.S. commerce.*

Section 301 is potentially the most useful instrument through which to counteract the tactics used by competitor nations in pursuit of their industrial policy objectives. While the president, working through the Office of the U.S. Trade Representative, is responsible for bringing actions under Section 301, such initiatives are made entirely at his discretion. The law defines no circumstances that make action mandatory. Section 301 was the basis for the tariff imposed upon Japan because of that nation's alleged failure to live up to the computer chip agreement. But overall, it has been used hardly at all, and the verdict of one analyst is that when trade laws depend on executive discretion, ''the result is paralysis.''

TRADE POLICY-MAKING SHOULD BE CENTRALIZED.

Trade matters are now the concern of the Commerce Department, the Office of the U.S. Trade Representative, which is part of the Executive Office of the President, and the U.S. International Trade Commission, an independent agency. The Treasury, State, and Defense departments also have influential roles in trade policy, and it is claimed that the special concerns of those departments—monetary, diplomatic, and military—take precedence in their reactions to trade proposals.

A proposal to replace this fragmented structure with a separate Department of International Trade and Industry is supported by such influential groups as the U.S. Chamber of Commerce and the National Association of Manufacturers. Proponents of the new department argue that a strong trade policy, which we do not now have, requires a strong and focused trade agency. They point out that while industrial policy and economic planning evoke strong negative reactions, there is public support for developing long-term foreign trade policy coordinated with domestic economic policies—which nobody in government is doing.

The 1983 report of the Labor-Industry Coalition for International Trade (the LICIT report) is consistent with the sentiment for more coordination, more thinking ahead. It recommended that information about the industrial policies of other countries and their potential effect on U.S. industries, trade, and employment be evaluated. Staff to undertake this is already in place in various departments and agencies, but their work is not coordinated and structured to do the defined job.

The report emphasizes that ongoing study will assure that damages are anticipated rather than merely reacted to after they happen. It cites the computer-chip industry as an example of the need for preemptive action. While the Japanese were developing their computer-chip capability in the mid-1970s, with government-directed and government-funded research, their markets were absolutely closed to American producers. Yet the United States did not take the action on behalf of that industry that was described in an earlier chapter until after the export onslaught from Japan had done enormous damage.

There is an interesting footnote to this issue of fragmentation in trade policy-making and implementation. Our foreign competitors maintain elaborate lobbying machinery in Washington. Their agents watch Congress with an eagle eye and move with lightning speed and amazing effectiveness when legislation or rulings threaten their interests. And we make things easier for them. As one critic of our present trade machinery put it: Because trade policy-making is so decentralized, the bargaining of foreign lobbyists is simplified. They can "shop around Washington for the best forum for their clients."

IMPORT BARRIERS TO PROTECT AMERICAN INDUSTRIES, WHETHER TARIFF OR NONTARIFF, SHOULD BE AVOIDED.

Protective tariffs raise the prices of imported goods and, by lessening their attractiveness, help American producers of those goods. The side effects of this protection, however, are obvious. To name just two: American consumers are hurt by protective tariffs. They lose the opportunity to buy the less expensive imported product. American producers who sell in foreign markets are also hurt by protective tariffs. If we place a tariff on Product X from Country A, it is inevitable that Country A will place a protective tariff on Product Z, a product that American producers have been selling in Country A. Take these recent examples: When the United States raised duties on cedar shakes and shingles from Canada, the Canadian retaliation was duties on American books, periodicals, and computer parts. When Spain entered the European Economic Community, it had to place a tariff on imported grain, which, it is claimed, will cause American farmers to lose $400 million in grain sales. In retal-

Members of the International Ladies' Garment Workers' Union demonstrating in Washington, D.C., in an effort to maintain import quotas.

iation, the United States announced 200 percent tariffs on a broad variety of European goods, including French wine, British gin, and Danish cheese.

Every administration from President Truman's on has wanted to keep Congress from passing protective-tariff legislation that would run counter to worldwide efforts to remove barriers to international trade. The amazing success of GATT (General Agreement on Trade and Tariffs) negotiations is evidenced by the figures. The general level of tariffs worldwide has fallen from 40 percent in the late 1940s to 5 percent today. And every administration from President Truman's on has used its powers under basic trade law to meet specific troublesome situations and thereby avoid a broader protectionist response from the legislature.

The Reagan years have witnessed many protectionist moves, with the result that about 22 percent of the imports that came into the country in 1986 were covered by some protection. That represents a widening of the protectionist umbrella from 12 percent in 1980 and 8 percent in 1975. The president did refuse protection to the shoe industry and did veto a textile-quota bill. But the United States has negotiated tough bilateral quota agreements with Hong Kong, Taiwan, South Korea, Japan, and other countries; raised duties on motorcycles; and placed curbs on machine tool imports from Taiwan, Japan, West Germany, and Switzerland.

The effect of quotas and voluntary-restraint agreements on consumers and producers is less widely understood than the effects of protective tariffs, but they are just as pernicious. For example, when the U.S./Japan computer-chips agreement established a floor price for Japanese chips, chip prices rose from $2 to $8 in August 1986. As a result, American manufacturers who use chips as a component in the products they manufacture found their costs of production higher. Those whose products compete with Japanese products were penalized; their Japanese competitors could buy cheap chips at home. Consumers, of course, ultimately paid the bill.

The voluntary-restraint agreement covering Japanese cars has cost U.S. car buyers billions of dollars. Protected against the threat of a flood of competing imports, American car prices could be raised, and Japanese exporters were under no challenge to lower prices. It has been estimated that 44,000 jobs were saved by the limitation on Japanese vehicles, but over a four-year period, price rises on American and Japanese cars cost American buyers $15.7 billion dollars, which works out to about $357,000 per job.

The effects of protective measures on consumers and nonprotected producers are indirect. The loss of a job because imports caused the closing of a plant is a direct effect. Closed plants and unemployed workers are highly visible; price tags carry no notation that "this price was raised because of a quota." So the pressure for protection is understandable, but there is fairly broad consensus that the zeal to avert it should not slacken. If foreign competition is really unfair, there are other ways to combat it. If the foreign competition is fair, there should be no interest in protecting inefficient U.S. producers who can't live with it.

THE GOVERNMENT SHOULD USE TRADE POLICY AS A MEANS OF FOSTERING BETTER LABOR CONDITIONS OVERSEAS.

The appalling conditions under which production is carried on in some of the newly industrializing countries of the Pacific rim are no secret. Stories detailing low wages, use of child labor, long hours, and unsanitary, even dangerous workplaces appear frequently in the media. There is legislation on the books that makes it possible to use trade policy to exert pressure on countries that tolerate those conditions.

The United States maintains a Generalized System of Preferences (GSP), a system developed ten years ago to help developing countries sell more. Under this system, products from 143 countries enter the United States duty-free. This, of course, gives them a price advantage in this market. Preferential treatment is subject to withdrawal for cause, and the Trade and Tariff Act of 1984 added worker-rights violations as a condition warranting such withdrawal. The president must, under that law, cancel the duty-free privileges of any country "that has not taken or is not taking steps to afford internationally recognized worker rights to workers." (Worker rights, as defined by International Labor Organization standards, include collective bargaining, minimum age for employment of children, acceptable minimum wage, maximum hours, safety and health protection.)

Those who favor the proposal stated above urge that coverage of the worker-rights provisions be extended beyond the GSP system, which covers only about 5 percent of imports. Those who oppose it argue that

(1) Worker rights provisions are a disguised form of protectionism. Penalizing foreign countries for low labor costs protects American inefficiency.

(2) The countries that would be subject to trade restrictions if internationally recognized worker rights were insisted upon would be seriously hurt, and among them are some countries that we do not want to hurt. We are pursuing other foreign policy goals there such as democracy, political stability, good relations with the United States.

(3) It is an attempt to impose our values on others.

THE IMPACT OF DEFENSE SPENDING ON MANUFACTURING SHOULD INFLUENCE ASSESSMENT OF NATIONAL PRIORITIES.

At one extreme on this highly controversial matter stand position statements like this one by Anthony Lewis, columnist for the *New York Times*.

> *The lesson of all this is plain. In our obsession with the Soviet threat we are doing ourselves severe economic damage. In our zeal to build ever more, newer, bigger weapons we are wasting the intellectual energy and physical substance needed for the real challenge this country faces. The challenge is economic: to make America competitive again, especially with the hard-working countries of East Asia. Responding to that is much more complicated politically, than denouncing the evil Soviet empire.*[30]

At the other extreme is the position that has dominated Washington thinking for the past ten years and was voiced repeatedly by former Secretary of Defense Caspar Weinberger, that it would indeed be desirable if we did not have to spend as much as we do on our defense, but because of the threat we face, we must spend whatever it takes to ensure that we do not endanger our liberty.

When discussions on this broad issue get down to specifics, mention of R & D is inevitable. Each year billions of dollars of expenditures by business and government fall into a category called *research and development (R & D)*. As the source of the innovation essential to improve old products and processes and create new ones, R & D is crucial to manufacturers' success.

Total U.S. expenditures for R & D exceed those of any developed country, but since 1964 R & D spending in France, West Germany, and Japan has been growing at a faster rate than in the United States. Many industry analysts agree that a disproportionate portion of R & D spending in the United States is done by the Pentagon, 55 percent in 1987. Those who take that position argue that only a small percentage of the Pentagon's R & D—2 percent in 1987—is spent on the kind of basic research that is likely to have applications outside the military. It is generally agreed, however, that military and space expenditures have provided substantial support for the aircraft and microelectronics industries.

Then there is the matter of the demands defense makes on human resources. The assertion is repeatedly made that top-flight scientists who might be contributing to R & D with direct impact on manufacturing are drawn off into government projects whose primary purposes are defense and security oriented. For example, the Defense Department and the National Security Agency hope to attract about one hundred eminent computer engineers to their Supercomputing Research Center. There they will work on the development of a breed of supercomputers called parallel processors that would expedite such computer-performed tasks as breaking codes or interpreting photographs taken from spy satellites.

Concern is expressed in some quarters that pursuit of Defense Department objectives has resulted in a technology drain from the United States. The Defense Department has carried on with Japan projects for the coproduction of airplanes. A 1982 General Accounting Office (GAO) report concluded that these programs had contributed substantially to the development of the Japanese aircraft industry. To ensure that the implications for American industry would be taken into consideration in the planning of future such coproduction projects, the GAO recommended that other departments, not just State and Defense, be involved in coproduction decisions.

Further discussion could be offered of actions urged upon the federal government to ameliorate the impact that loss of competiveness has had on workers and communities: federal legislation requiring advance notice of plant closings; federal involvement in job training programs. And still further discussion could be offered about broad goals the government should pursue that are directly relevant to American competitiveness: an increase in consumer saving that will foster investment; an improvement in educational achievement that will ensure a quality labor resource.

And finally, two inescapable mandates for the federal government must be recited. First, the United States must put its economic house in order, get control of its annual budget deficits and mounting debt. Failing that, nothing that it does specifically about competitiveness will work in the long run.

Second, the United States must view its weakened competitive position as part of a much bigger picture and act accordingly. U.S. growth has slowed, world growth has slowed, and the equation is inexorable: Economic growth slower than population growth equals declining living standards. In the good old days the United States could serve as locomotive for the world to crank up economic growth. Now it will take a partnership of the world's three leading industrial powers—the United States, West Germany, and Japan—to provide leadership for world growth. Failing that, however successful we may be as competitors, we will all slide down together.

GLOSSARY

Antitrust laws: U.S. laws designed to maintain competition by forbidding specific kinds of contacts or connections among the companies in an industry.

Capital: an individual's or company's income-producing assets.

Capital goods: man-made physical goods used to produce other goods: plants, tools, machinery for example.

COLA clauses: cost-of-living-adjustment provisions in labor contracts guaranteeing wage increases to keep up with price increases.

Conglomerate: a business enterprise that produces a wide variety of goods and/or services.

Constant dollars: dollars with the same purchasing power. A specific year always accompanies this phrase: constant 1982 dollars, constant 1985 dollars, etc. Constant dollars are used to make comparisons over time, say, average hourly wage of steel workers over the last twenty years. The average hourly wage of steel workers in 1976, 1977, 1978, etc., for example, would be translated into 1982 or 1985 dollars of equivalent purchasing power.

Cost-plus contracts: government/business contracts that guarantee the providers of goods or services payments large enough to cover the cost of providing the goods or services plus profit of an agreed percentage.

Current account: the international balance sheet that reflects all the movements of funds (other than capital investments) into and out of a country in a given period of time.

Current dollars: dollars with today's purchasing power at today's prices.

Debtor nation: a nation whose government, businesses, and citizens collectively owe more to foreign creditors than is due them from foreign debtors.

133

Deindustrialization: a decline in the relative importance of manufacturing in the economic activity of a country.

Dumping: selling products abroad for less than it costs to produce them, or at less than "fair value."

Economic growth: persistent, long-term increases in per capita income.

Exchange rate: the price of one country's currency expressed in terms of another country's currency.

Goods: tangible things which satisfy human wants.

Gross national product: the dollar value of all the goods and services produced in a year.

High-tech industry: manufacturing involving the production or use of advanced or sophisticated methods or devices, especially in the fields of electronics and computers.

Index number: a figure that discloses the relative change, if any, of prices, costs, or some other variable between one period of time and another period of time that has been selected as the base period and assigned the index number 100.

Industrial policy: intervention of government in the economy to promote—or allow the decline of—specifically targeted industries.

Industry: a specific kind of manufacturing or production such as the steel industry, the furniture industry, the lighting fixtures industry. The term is also used as a synonym for manufacturing as contrasted with agriculture, mining, trade, transport, finance.

Investment: the purchase of income-producing property, tangible (a factory, an apartment house, a machine used in production) or intangible (stocks, bonds).

Invisible exports: transactions other than sale of merchandise that cause funds to flow into a country.

Invisible imports: transactions other than purchase of merchandise that cause funds to flow out of a country.

Labor force: the total number of workers employed or looking for work.

Lobbying: efforts by businesses and other interest groups to influence legislation or other government action relevant to their concerns.

Market share: the percentage of the total sales of a product customarily made by one seller of that product.

Median wage: the wage in the middle. Of all the individuals employed, half receive more than the median wage, half receive less.

Multinational: a corporation organized under the laws of one nation that does business in many nations.

Nominal exports/imports: the value of exports or imports in current dollars.

Nominal wages: money wages; the amounts received in current dollars.

Out-sourcing: the business practice of purchasing parts and components from outside suppliers rather than producing them in-house.

134

Productivity: the relationship between input (the amount of labor and capital used) and output (the amount produced) in production. The most commonly used measure of productivity is output of product per work-hour.

Protectionist measures: legislation or administrative actions that have the effect of restricting imports, such as protective tariffs, quotas, voluntary restraint agreements.

Protective tariff: a tax placed on an imported commodity to cause a rise in its price to a level that protects American producers of that commodity from competing with a cheaper foreign product.

Quality circles: small groups of workers within a factory or plant charged with responsibility for improving their own performance.

Quota: (as related to international trade) a limit placed by Country A on the quantity of Commodity X that may be exported to A by Country B.

R & D: research and development; expenditures by governments and businesses for research and development aimed at fostering innovation—new products and new ways of producing.

Real exports/imports: the volume (tons, pounds, units) of exports and imports.

Real wages: what can be bought with money wages.

Restructuring: as used in discussion of American competitiveness, the term means changes in the structure, composition, and organization of corporations—selling off of subsidiaries, dropping or consolidation of departments or divisions, merging of units and the like.

Service sector: those business and government enterprises that render services rather than produce goods.

Smokestack industries: traditional, old-line, "heavy" industries such as steel, automobiles, machine tools.

Standard of living: the amount of necessities, comforts, and luxuries which individuals or nations are accustomed to enjoy.

Subsidies: as used in discussion of international trade, subsidies are payments by governments to producers based on the number of specified products they export, thus enabling the exporters to offer lower prices to overseas customers.

Trade balance: the relationship between merchandise imports and merchandise exports. When a country's exports exceed its imports it has a trade surplus; when its imports exceed its exports, it has a trade deficit.

Trade weighted dollar value index number: a figure that reflects change in the trade-weighted average of U.S. exchange rates with its ten leading trade partners. (See *weighted average*.)

Two-tier wage systems: wage systems under which newly hired workers, or workers recalled from layoffs, are paid at a lower rate than current workers.

Voluntary restraint agreement: As an alternative to the imposition of quotas, bargaining sessions between exporting nations and U.S. trade officials produce agreements like this: Country A agrees that it will not permit its steel producers to export more than x tons of steel per year to the United States.

Weighted average: An average is the sum of a group of numbers divided by the number of items in the group. A weighted average reflects the relative importance of the numbers entering into the average. For example, a teacher computing pupils' averages might consider a full-period test five times as important as each of five brief quizzes. So she multiplies the mark earned on the full-period test by five, adds it to the five quiz marks, and divides by ten. The result is a weighted average.

SOURCE NOTES

CHAPTER ONE

1. The so-called 1971 Peterson Report on a study, initiated by President Richard Nixon, of the competitive position of the United States.

CHAPTER TWO

2. Economic Report of the President (January 1987). Table B-105. p. 365.
3. Robert Kuttner, "The Theory Gap on the Trade Gap," *New York Times* (Jan. 17, 1988), sec. 3, p. 1.
4. Telephone call. Department of Commerce, Bureau of Economic Analysis. (June 9, 1988).

CHAPTER THREE

5. For example: Barry Bluestone and Bennett Harrison, *The Deindustrialization of America* (New York: Basic Books, 1982).
6. C. Jackson Grayson, Jr., head of the American Productivity Center in Houston. *New York Times* (Feb. 21, 1988), sec. 3, p. 6.

CHAPTER FOUR

7. Walter B. Wriston, *Risk & Other Four-Letter Words* (New York: Harper & Row, 1986), p. 152.
8. David Platt, Chrysler Corporation, quoted in the *New York Times* (May 1, 1987), sec. D, p. 4.

9. Louis Uchitelle, "Japan Winning in Auto Parts," *New York Times* (May 1, 1987), sec. D, p. 4.
10. Stephen Marris, cited in: Barnaby J. Feder, "Where the High Yen Hurts," *New York Times* (May 18, 1987), sec. D, p. 5.
11. Tom Peters. *Thriving on Chaos: Handbook for a Management Revolution* (New York: Alfred A. Knopf, 1987), p. 3.

CHAPTER FIVE

12. Deputy Treasury Secretary Richard G. Darman, quoted in: Richard Fly, "A backlash against business is building—and the Democrats know it," *Business Week* (April 6, 1987), p. 49.
13. Tom Peters. *Thriving on Chaos: Handbook for a Management Revolution* (New York: Alfred A. Knopf, 1987).

CHAPTER SIX

14. Brock Yates. *The Decline and Fall of the American Automobile Industry* (New York: Empire Books, 1983).
15. William J. Hampton and James R. Norman, "General Motors: What Went Wrong," *Business Week* (March 16, 1987), pp. 102–107.
16. Jeremy Main. "Ford's Drive for Quality," *Fortune* (April 18, 1983), p. 62.

CHAPTER SEVEN

17. *Fortune* (October 1966), p. 135, quoted in: Walter Adams and James W. Brock. *The Bigness Complex: Industry, Labor and Government in the American Economy* (New York: Pantheon Books, 1986), p. 58.
18. William J. Abernathy, Kim B. Clark, and Alan M. Kantrow, *Industrial Renaissance: Producing a Competitive Future for America* (New York: Basic Books, 1983), p. 122.
19. Seymour Melman, *Profits Without Production* (New York: Alfred A. Knopf, 1983), p. 9.
20. Gene Bylinsky, "The Race to the Automatic Factory," *Fortune* (Feb. 21, 1983), p. 52.
21. Emily T. Smith and Jo Ellen Davis, "Our Life Has Changed," *Business Week* (April 6, 1987), pp. 94–95.

CHAPTER EIGHT

22. Robert D. Hershey, Jr., "Small Manufacturers Head Revival," *New York Times* (Feb. 11, 1988), sec. D, p. 1.

CHAPTER NINE

23. Brock Yates, *The Decline and Fall of the American Automobile Industry* (New York: Empire Books, 1983), p. 232.
24. Deputy Assistant Secretary of Commerce James P. Moore, quoted in: Steve Lohr, "U.S. Companies Woo Europe," *New York Times* (Nov. 13, 1987), sec. D, p. 1.
25. Benjamin C. Duke, "The Truth Will Come Out in the Wash," *New York Times* (Sept. 21, 1986).

CHAPTER TEN

26. William Glaberson, "An Uneasy Alliance in Smokestack U.S.A.," *New York Times* (March 13, 1988), sec. D, p. 1.
27. Martin F. Payson of Jackson, Lewis, Schnitzler and Krupman, a New York labor law firm for management, quoted in: William Serrin, "Industries, in Shift, Aren't Letting Strikes Stop Them," *New York Times* (Sept. 30, 1986), sec. A, p. 18.
28. Institute for Labor Economics and Research, *What's Wrong with the U.S. Economy? A Popular Guide for the Rest of Us* (Boston: South End Press, 1982), p. 355. Figures from this study, given in the text, cited in: Walter Russell Mead, *Mortal Splendor: the American Empire in Transition* (Boston: Houghton Mifflin), 1987.

CHAPTER ELEVEN

29. *International Trade, Industrial Policies, and the Future of American Industry.* The Labor-Industry Coalition for International Trade. (April 1983), p. 13.
30. Anthony Lewis, "The Wrong War," *New York Times* (April 7, 1987), sec. A, p. 35.

INDEX

Agriculture, 29, 31, 37
Application-specific integrated circuits (ASICs), 85, 87
AT&T, 57, 85, 88
Automobile industry: employment in, 29–31, 107–108; foreign competition in, 17, 26, 61–63, 127; multinational operations of, 48–49; productivity gains, 63–69; recalls, 92

Banks, international, 12, 15, 43, 46
Brazil, 13, 24–25, 48, 114; industrial policy in, 116, 118–119
Budget deficit, 16–17, 22, 131

Canada, 24–25, 36, 50, 116, 124
Chrysler, 48, 62, 63, 108
Communications industry, 15, 46, 93–94
Competitiveness, 131; as Congressional issue, 13; and labor, 105–109; productivity and, 34–35; quality control and, 92–93; successes in, 56–57, 93–94

Computer-assisted design and computer-assisted manufacturing (CAD/CAM), 78, 100
Continuous casting, 71 72
"Corpocracy," 56
Cost-of-living adjustment (COLA), 108
Currency markets, 10, 21
Customer service, 97–98

Deindustrialization, 17–19, 28, 31, 32
Dollar, value of, 10, 38, 121; exchange rates, 19–21, 24–26, 50; and trade deficit, 22–23, 28; trade-weighted, 21–22, 24
Dumping, 84, 120–121, 134
Dynamic random-access memory (DRAM), 83–84, 85

Eastman Kodak Co., 50, 97
Economy, domestic: foreign competition in, 12–13, 17; government intervention in, 116; job classifications in, 29, 30; new jobs in, 112–113.

141

Efficiency, 34–35
Employment: exports and, 27; job classifications, 29, 30; in manufacturing, 29–31, 32–33. *See also* Labor
Europe, 10, 13, 114, 115, 119
Exchange rates, currency, 19, 21–24, 50, 134
Exports: difficulties of marketing, 94–97; invisible, 15; "lost," 52–53; real and nominal, 26–27; of semiconductors, 84–85; value of the dollar and, 23, 26; volume of, 16–19, 27, 28

Federal Reserve, 21, 24
Flexible manufacturing (FM) systems, 78–79, 80; and labor, 100
Ford Motor Co., 48, 57, 62–63, 65, 66–69, 102, 107–108
France, 24, 36, 116–117, 130

General Agreement on Trade and Tariffs (GATT), 126
General Electric Co., 50, 97, 101
Generalized System of Preferences (GSP), 128
General Motors Corp., 48, 57, 62–66, 79, 108
"Globalization of technology," 47
Global village, 46
Great Britain, 24
Gross national product, 32, 36, 134

Hong Kong, 13, 24–25, 50, 114, 126

IBM, 53, 85, 86, 88, 101
Imports: invisible, 15; machine tool, 80; preference for, 51–52; prices of, 26; and protectionism, 125, 126–127; rates, 26–27;
value of the dollar and, 23, 26; volume of, 16–19, 28, 75. *See also* Protectionism
Industrial policies, 116–120, 123
Insurance industry, 15
INTEL Corporation, 85

Japan, 10–12, 13, 36, 81, 130; automobile industry, 49, 62–63, 93, 127; and dumping, 121; exports to, 51, 96–97; imports from, 15–16, 26, 49–50, 78, 80, 126–127; industrial policy in, 115, 116, 117–118, 119; labor-management relations method, 66, 98–100; semiconductor industry, 84, 122, 123, 126–127; U.S. companies in, 48, 96; wages in, 114; yen, value of the dollar against, 24–26, 50, 51
Job classifications, 29, 30

Kennedy, John F., 12
Korean War, 10–12

Labor: and competitiveness, 102, 105–109, 127–128; costs, 72, 113; and FM systems, 79; force, 31; income, 109–110, 114; in Japan, 66, 98–100, 118; job security, 102, 107–108; management relations, 66–69, 74–75, 100–103; part-time and temporary, 110–113; strikes, 108–109; worker rights, 127–128; work teams, 101, 108. *See also* Management, corporate; Wages
Labor-Industry Coalition for International Trade (LICIT), 123
Labor-management participation teams (LMPTs), 74–75
LDI Manufacturing Co., 89

Lewis, Anthony, 129

Machine tool industry, 11; and foreign competition, 80, 126; Japanese, 118; technological innovation in, 77–79, 97, 100
Management, corporate: failures of, 57–58, 61; labor relations, 66–69, 74–75, 100–103; and labor strikes, 109
Manufacturing: corporate management of, 55–59, 61; and customer service, 97–98; defense spending for, 129–130; employment in, 29–31, 32–33, 108, 112; goods, 12, 28, productivity in, 38, 40, 41; quality control in, 91–93; technological innovation in, 77–79
Marshall Plan, 10–12, 116
Mexico, 13, 24–25, 51, 116; wages in, 106, 114
Multinational corporations, 10, 44–48, 50, 52–53

Natural gas industry, 43
New United Motor Manufacturing Inc., 66, 67
Nixon, Richard M., 12
Nominal exports and imports, 26–27

Oxygen furnace, 71–72

Part-time jobs, 110–112, 113
Pension plans, 112
Power-generating machinery, 17, 119
Productivity: and competitiveness, 34–36, 66, 113; at Ford's Louisville plant, 67–69; measuring, 35–37
Profit sharing, 102, 108

Protectionism, 75, 80, 135, 120–122; effects of, 23–24, 84, 124–127; worker rights as, 128. See also Imports; Tariffs

Quality control, 91–93, 101
Quotas, import, 125, 126

Radios, transistor, 76–77
Reagan, Ronald, 56, 80, 81, 126
Real estate, 26
Real exports and imports, 26–27
Research and development, 129–130, 135
Restructuring, corporate, 56–57, 135

Securities, 22, 57–58
Sematech, 85–87, 88
Semiconductor industry, 45; and foreign competition, 32, 83–85; Japanese, 122, 123, 126–127
Service sector, 29, 31, 32, 37–38, 112
Shoe industry, 17, 126
Silicon Valley, 32, 83
Singapore, 13, 24–25, 51, 106, 114
South Korea, 13, 24–25, 50–51, 114, 116, 126
Soviet Union, 81, 129
Spain, 124
Steel industry, 35, 71–76, 107
Strikes, 108–109
Subsidies, 120, 121. See also Industrial policies
Superconductivity, government and, 81–82
Switzerland, 80; import restrictions on, 126

Taiwan, 13, 24–25, 50–51, 80, 114, 126

143

Targeting, 121–122. *See also* Industrial policies

Tariffs: effects of, 124–127; on imported steel, 75; and Japan, 84, 118, 122, 123. *See also* Protectionism

Technology, 10, 15, 47; in automobile industry, 65–66; communications, 46, 93–94; and industry, 31–32, 100, 117; machine tool, 77–79; steel industry and, 71–74, 76; superconductor, 81–82

Televisions, manufacture of, 49–50

Texas Instruments, 46, 85

Textile industry, 17, 78, 93–94, 126

Toyota, 48, 66, 67

Trade: partners, 21, 24; unfair practices, 120–122; U.S. policy, 122–124; world, 9–13, 46, 115

Trade deficit: overseas production and, 52–53; and value of the dollar, 22–23; volume of, 12–13, 16–19, 26–28

Trade-weighted value of the dollar index number, 21–22, 24

Treasury bills and bonds, 22

Unemployment, 109, 127

Unfair trade practices, 120–122

Unions. *See* Labor

United Auto Workers (UAW), 68–69, 102, 107–108

United States: Commerce Department. 28, 52, 94, 120, 122; Congress, 13, 23–24, 126; Current Account, 15, 133; Defense Department, 78, 80, 87, 130–131; defense spending, 74, 129–130; economic dominance of, 9–12; Federal Reserve Board, 21, 24; foreign policy, 128; General Accounting Office (GAO), 130–131; government, and business, 75, 80, 84, 115–116, 119–131; International Trade Commission (ITC), 120–121, 123; Labor Department, 74, 109, 113; Marshall Plan, 10–12; national security, 32, 84; National Security Agency, 130; productivity in, 36–38; quota agreements, 126; share of world exports, 12; State Department, 131; steel production, 71–72; Trade Act of 1974, 122; Trade and Tariff Act of 1984, 128; Treasury Department, 22; as world's largest debtor, 17

United Steelworkers of America, 107

USX Corp., 74, 107

Vietnam War, 10–12

Volkswagen AG, 62

Volvo, 105

Wages: concessions, 66, 75; failure to improve, 32, 113–114; in motor manufacturing, 106; in newly created jobs, 109–112; for overseas labor, 127; and shift to service economy, 32; tier systems, 107. *See also* Labor

Weinberger, Caspar, 129

West Germany, 24–25, 36, 130; imports from, 126; industrial policy in, 116, 117; machine tool production in, 78, 80

Westinghouse Electric, 50, 101

Worker rights, 127–128

Work teams, 101, 108

World trade, 9–13, 46, 115

World War II, 10–12

Xerox, 101